Toni Cavanagh Johnson, PhD

Sexual, Physical, and Emotional Abuse in Out-of-Home Care: Prevention Skills for At-Risk Children

D0166675

Pre-publication
REVIEWS,
COMMENTARIES,
EVALUATIONS . . .

"**T**his book is a comprehensive curriculum that provides step-by-step instruction for clinicians in out-of-home care. This specialized curriculum is long overdue! It is an essential tool for all clinicians working with children who live out-of-home. The therapeutic value of this book will benefit many children."

Debra Manners, LCSW
Associate Executive Director,
The Sycamores,
Altadena, California

Haworth Maltreatment and Trauma Press, Inc.

Sexual, Physical, and Emotional Abuse in Out-of-Home Care

Prevention Skills for At-Risk Children

Sexual, Physical, and Emotional Abuse in Out-of-Home Care

Prevention Skills for At-Risk Children

Toni Cavanagh Johnson, PhD
and Associates

Haworth Maltreatment and Trauma Press
An Imprint of The Haworth Press, Inc.
New York • London

Published by

Haworth Maltreatment and Trauma Press, an imprint of The Haworth Press, Inc., 10 Alice Street, Binghamton, NY 13904-1580

Cover design by Marylouise E. Doyle.

Library of Congress Cataloging-in-Publication Data

Johnson, Toni Cavanagh.
    Sexual, physical, and emotional abuse in out-of-home care: Prevention skills for at-risk children/ Toni Cavanagh Johnson.
       p. cm.
    Includes bibliographical references and index.
    ISBN 0-7890-0193-4 (alk. paper)
    1. Child abuse–Prevention–Problems, exercises, etc. 2. Children–Institutional care. 3. Group counseling for children. 4. Group counseling. I. Title.
RJ507.A29J64 1997
618.92′858223–dc20
                                                         96-36223
                                                              CIP

This curriculum was written after years of working as a clinician and consultant with children in residential treatment facilities, group, and foster homes. Throughout these years the children have helped me to understand what it is like to live "alone" without their families. For many of these children it is a time of great fear, despair, shame, and guilt. A number of these children feel it was a big mistake to tell about the abuse in their homes because of how they feel in out-of-home care. This curriculum is dedicated to these children and all of the caring adults who nurture them.

Everything that is said to a child and everything the child experiences contributes to that child's self-worth. The intensity of this effect is magnified a hundred times with vulnerable children in out-of-home care.

ABOUT THE AUTHOR

Toni Cavanagh Johnson, PhD, is a licensed clinical psychologist in private practice in South Pasadena, California. She has been working in the field of child abuse for 19 years as a researcher, trainer, and clinician. For the past 11 years, she has provided highly specialized treatment for children who are under 12 and have sexual behavior problems. Her research on boys and girls who molest other children has been published in *Child Abuse and Neglect* and her treatment program for these children appeared in the *Journal of Interpersonal Violence.* The author of the *Child Sexuality Curriculum for Abused Children and Their Parents* and *Treatment Exercises for Abused Children and Children with Sexual Behavior Problems,* she is the developer of a game for sexually abused and sexually agressive children and a game for victims of incest. Dr. Johnson is also co-author of the book *Sexualized Children: The Assessment and Treatment of Sexualized Children and Children Who Molest.*

Dr. Johnson has lectured on child abuse throughout the United States and in Australia, New Zealand, South America, Europe, and Canada. She provides consultation to protective service workers, mental health professionals, attorneys, the police, probation officers, and the courts in the area of sexual victimization and perpetration.

CONTENTS

Associates   **x**

Acknowledgments   **xi**

Chapter 1. Introduction   **1**

Purpose   2
Content   3
Implementing the Curriculum   4
How to Use the Curriculum   5
Language Usage   6
Policies in Out-of-Home Care   7
Group Members   7
Group Leaders and Cofacilitators   8
Imparting Personal Information to the Children   11
Supervision   11
Feedback to All Caregivers Who Work
     with the Children in Each Group   12
Length of Group Meetings   12
Group Size   13
Behavior Management in the Group   13
Structuring the Group Time   14
Group Process   15
Allegations of Abuse or Misuse   16
Keeping the Material from Each Session   17
Individual, Family Sessions, and Multifamily Groups   17
The Curriculum and Therapy   18
Issues May Arise That Will Need Intervention   18
Ordering Supplementary Materials   19

Chapter 2. Exploring Communication   **21**

Objectives   21
Rationale and Purpose   21

Exercise One: A Continuum of Communication I   22
Exercise Two: A Continuum of Communication II   25
Exercise Three: Harmful and Hurtful Communications I   29
Exercise Four: Harmful and Hurtful Communications II   31

Chapter 3. Exploring Touch   **35**

Objectives   35
Rationale and Purpose   36
General Instructions   38
Exercise One: A Continuum of Touch I   39
Exercise Two: A Continuum of Touch II   41
Exercise Three: Sexual Touch–A Continuum
   from Comforting and Soothing
   to Harmful and Hurtful and Violent   44

**Chapter 4. Differentiating Between Sexual Play
and Sexual Abuse**   **49**

Objectives   49
Rationale and Purpose   49
Exercise One: Differentiating Sexual Play
   from Sexual Abuse   51
Exercise Two: Let's Talk About Touching   54

Chapter 5. Personal Space   **55**

Objectives   55
Rationale and Purpose   55
General Instructions   58
Exercise One: Personal Comfort Zones   58
Exercise Two: Space Invaders   60

Chapter 6. Sexual Knowledge   **63**

Objectives   63
Rationale and Purpose   63
Exercise One: Body Parts   64
Exercise Two: The Function of the Sexual Parts   66
Exercise Three: Where Do I Come From?   67
Exercise Four: As You Grow Up   68

Chapter 7. Prevention of Sexual Misuse or Abuse   **69**

   Objectives   69
   Rationale and Purpose   69
   Exercise One: Learning About Prevention Through Plays   71
   Exercise Two: Grooming and Threats   75
   Exercise Three: Being Alert   78
   Exercise Four: Figuring Out the Rules   80
   Exercise Five: Helping Other Children   82

References   **83**

Appendix A: Children's Sexual Behaviors   **85**

   Natural and Healthy Sexual Behaviors   85
   Twenty Characteristics of Problematic Sexual Behavior   86

Appendix B: How to Use the Behavior Chart   **95**

   Objectives   95
   Rationale and Purpose   95
   Using Behavioral Charts   96

Appendix C: Worksheets   **105**

Index   **115**

Associates

**Clinical Staff
at The Sycamores**

Lisa Buchwald, MSW
Richard Croyt, MFCC
Andrea Farb, MSW
Anna Maria Guerra, PhD
Joelle Hunnewell, LCSW
Cynthia Kelly, MSW
Debra Manners, LCSW
Stan Rushing, MA

**Clinical Staff
Hillsides Home for Children**

Sabrina Luza, MSW
Lisa Manzo, MSW

Acknowledgments

It has been a great pleasure to write this curriculum because of all of the people I have met along the way. The children stand out as the greatest contributors to my understanding of some of the drawbacks to living outside your family in the care of the government. I want to especially thank Ebony A., Angel B., Melissa C., Meagan C., Thomas C., Donna D., Kim E., Daniel F., Nancy K., Randy K., Karen L., Jessica M., Arthur O., Shelisa R., Terra R., Alison S., and Christine S. Strength, wisdom, courage, and a will to make it in the world characterize these children. With odds tilted against them, they march forward with a diligence and perseverance few of us outside this "system" ever need to muster. They are an inspiration to those of us who were not abused and who lived at home with a nurturing family to support us.

This curriculum is the culmination of staff consultation and clinical work with children in out-of-home care. I worked on this curriculum while consulting to The Sycamores, a residential treatment program in Altadena, California. Lisa Buchwald, MSW, Richard Croyt, MFCC, Andrea Farb, MSW, Anna Maria Guerra, PhD, David B. Hickel, PhD, Joelle Hunnewell, LCSW, Cynthia Kelly, MSW, Debra Manners, LCSW, and Stan Rushing, MA at The Sycamores used the modules with five groups of boys and together we made changes, additions, and deletions. Their assistance was crucial in understanding some of the challenges in working with staff, social workers, administrators, and children in this highly sensitive area of abuse. The introduction to this work was formulated from conversations with them and with the social workers, Sabrina Luza, MSW and Lisa Manzo, MSW at Hillsides Home for Children in Pasadena, California. Sabrina and Lisa also co-led with me all of the exercises with several groups of preteen girls. Geri Monohan, Sheryl Castleberry, Lucy Garabedian, Aida Khoudaghoulian, Marsha Wilson, and Kathy Mahony are caregivers at Hillsides who participated in the groups with the children and gave me feedback about their perception of the exercises. They made excellent observations that are incorporated in the final product. Doing the curriculum with them was a powerful experience that I will always remember. I greatly thank them for persevering with me even when it was tough.

Vicki Henderson at The Children's Foundation in Vancouver, British Columbia generously agreed to use the curriculum as it was being developed with some of the boys in the Esther Irwin Home and provide me with their perspective. Liam Grayer and Chris Dawkins, both caregivers, and a consultant, John Taylor, helped me to see the need for additional background material and knowledge to support the use of the curriculum by the staff. Some of the introductory material comes from their experience. I am very grateful to them for providing me with this very helpful feedback.

Chapter 1

Introduction

In the 1980s there was a growing understanding that children were at risk for sexual abuse. In response, many programs that had previously been developed to teach children self-protection began to focus more heavily on sexual abuse (Wurtele and Miller-Perrin, 1992). It took many years to devise effective programs. As content was being written some program developers asked the sex offenders directly about their modus operandi and how they felt they could have been prevented from offending children (Elliot et al., 1995; Budin and Johnson, 1989). Almost all programs were provided in school settings. Initially there was not much research on the effectiveness of these programs but recent research indicates that children do learn concepts which are helpful in preventing victimization (Wurtele et al., 1992; Finkelhor et al., 1995; Finkelhor and Dziuba-Leatherman, 1995). Evaluation of prevention programs indicates that more should be included about bullies, as this is very salient and useful information and therefore catches children's attention (Finkelhor et al., 1995). Additionally, it has been found that parents are very effective teachers and that parental participation in programs increases the child's learning and follow through (Finkelhor et al., 1995).

As the knowledge about the sexual abuse of children increased, it was discovered that more than half of all children in out-of-home care had been sexually abused (Hargrave, 1991). Increasingly, residential facilities were finding children engaged in sexual behaviors with one another (Navarre, 1983; Hargrave, 1991). Protocols were developed for reporting abuse that occurred between children or by adults to children in institutions (Navarre, 1983; Hargrave, 1991). Bloom (1992) describes an institutional response when there are allegations that a staff person has abused a child. Prevention of abuse in institutions has been a major issue of concern (Gil, 1982). Yet, in an extensive literature search, no prevention programs specifically developed for the prevention of abuse to children or by children in out-of-home care was found.

Sexual, Physical, and Emotional Abuse in Out-of-Home Care was developed using information from children on how they abuse others and how it would be best to prevent them from doing it. Children were used to test the program and aid in its development. Participation in this prevention program is differ-ent from all others as all potential people who could engage in abusing are trained together in the techniques of how not to be abused. The learning of the children is expected to be increased as the caregivers and social workers in out-of-home care are participants in the training as are the biological parents (if the children are to return home).

PURPOSE

The major focus of the curriculum is to bring out into the open current or past sexually, physically, or emotionally abusive or offen-sive behaviors between children, or between children and caregiv-ers (see definition of caregivers below) and to prevent future vic-timization. The other major focus is to increase respectful and nurturing interactions between caregivers and children. This will encourage positive attachments for the children who feel abandoned by their families and alone in out-of-home care. The residual effect of the curriculum is happier and healthier children and caregivers.

The exercises assist children and caregivers to understand their rights and the rights of others in all out-of-home care facilities including RTCs (Residential Treatment Centers), group, and foster homes. It offers children and caregivers healthy concepts regarding touching, communication, and boundaries. It provides prevention exercises to help children identify all types of abuse by adults, adolescents, and children, both in and outside their living situation.

It is essential that children feel comfortable after they have been removed from their own homes. Children who have been removed from their families may have been abused. Abused children have an increased risk for further abuse. This curriculum attempts to provide children with a broad understanding of their rights and the rights of others related to touch, communication, and boundaries therefore decreasing their risk for further abuse.

The curriculum can be used for caregiver training, or caregivers and children can do the curriculum together. See the sections on Implementing the Curriculum and How to Use the Curriculum. This curriculum is also very useful for working with the children's families, either in family sessions or multifamily groups.

CONTENT

Generally, children in out-of-home care have been maltreated in many different ways. These children need large amounts of guidance to assure their safety and healthy growth. Among the issues that need to be addressed with children in out-of-home facilities are their rights and responsibilities related to their bodies. When children have been sexually, physically, and/or emotionally abused or neglected, they often do not have good self-protection skills. We make assumptions that all children know when someone is violating them. If they have not been taught or cannot model their behavior on the people who raised them, they often do not know.

The curriculum begins with many exercises in which the children learn about communication. These concepts are taught on a continuum, from comforting and soothing to harmful and hurtful. Children and caregivers talk together, giving examples of all parts of each continuum. Verbal communication is differentiated from nonverbal communication. Children and caregivers work on expressing their thoughts and feelings without hurting others. They also practice responding to harmful and hurtful comments.

A continuum of types of touch is discovered with children discussing examples from present and past experience. Space violations as well as emotional and physical boundary violations are examined between children and between children and caregivers. Children and caregivers work together on how to differentiate between sexual play and sexual abuse between children. Four sessions on child sexuality are included to provide some very basic knowledge and to encourage questioning and discussion about sexual material in a nonthreatening place. An enormous amount of misinformation is held by children who have come from abusive homes. Finding the misinformation and distortions regarding sexuality has a positive effect on children. The last module teaches prevention of abuse. This module is often the favorite as the children enjoy doing the plays which are a major focus of the prevention work.

Several exercises provide the children the opportunity to create something to benefit other children such as pamphlets, videos, or posters.

IMPLEMENTING THE CURRICULUM

Depending on what kind of out-of-home facility (RTC, group home, or foster home) is utilizing the curriculum, some planning will be helpful. The person in charge of the out-of-home facility will decide how the curriculum will be used, with whom, and when. Some sessions of the curriculum can be used to train staff before they begin to work with children or some parts of the curriculum can be used with children and caregivers together in some cottages or the whole curriculum can be used with all caregivers and children in all cottages. Whichever avenue is decided upon, all of the caregivers who will be involved in the implementation should be given an opportunity to read, comment on, and then discuss the curriculum before its implementation. If there are reservations or concerns caregivers have regarding the curriculum, these can be handled before implementation.

It can be highly beneficial to use the curriculum as a training tool for caregivers independent of the children. If the curriculum is first done with the caregivers together, they can use it more effectively in the cottage. As the vocabulary and method of interacting with children and each other may be different than what has occurred previously, this introduction will give the caregivers time to learn. It may be valuable to have some of the administrators involved in the training also. All of the exercises will not be necessary, but at least one or two from the communication, touch, and personal space modules will be excellent training. Issues will arise in these sessions that will assist the caregivers to clarify the rules and ways of interacting with the children.

If the curriculum will be used with caregivers and children together, a point person or leader is needed to spearhead the use of the curriculum. This person should work with the person in charge of the home to decide on implementation. As time and energy must be allocated to plan and have the groups, the backing of the owners or top administrators is important.

HOW TO USE THE CURRICULUM

Most people use the curriculum from beginning to end. This takes approximately 20 sessions or 20 weeks. The curriculum is built so that the material flows throughout each module, yet each exercise in a module does not have to be done. The modules can be done in the order presented or can be switched around. The designated leader along with some caregivers may want to read the objectives and the rationale and purpose for each of the modules to determine which they want to do and the order in which they want to proceed. Each group of children will need emphasis in different areas, hence, selection will be group specific.

When the material to be covered has been selected, the designated person should read all the sessions thoroughly before starting. In this way he or she will be sure of the material to be covered. All caregivers who will participate should have the opportunity to read the exercise prior to being in the session. It is most helpful if the caregivers who will be in the session can meet to discuss the exercise prior to its implementation.

It can be very beneficial for the language related to the communication and touch continua to become part of the cottage language. When caregivers and children are familiar with the different types of communication and touch, they can identify them in the cottage. This will make their communication more meaningful. "What you are saying sounds 'harmful and hurtful,' is that what you want?"

LANGUAGE USAGE

When the term "children" is used it refers to children and adolescents. While the author does not see adolescents as children, it seemed overly burdensome to state "children and adolescents" throughout the curriculum. The term adolescent alone is less representative of all children than the term children for adolescents. The reader should substitute the expanded statement "children and adolescents" when reading "children."

When the term "caregivers" is used in the curriculum, it refers to all persons who interact with the children in out-of-home care, e.g., counselors, social workers, administrators, school personnel, line staff in the cottages, substitute caregivers, part-time caregivers, volunteers, etc.

The term "cottage" is used to refer to the living areas of children in out-of-home care. Out-of-home care is used as a short term to refer to both residential treatment centers which may have a large number of children, group homes which will generally have four to eight children, and foster homes.

POLICIES IN OUT-OF-HOME CARE

Each out-of-home setting defines its rules about hugs, restraints, caregivers in rooms, bathroom privacy, applying medication to the genitals, caregivers taking children on outings, restraints, and other issues that arise about touch and boundaries. It is most helpful when children and caregivers are clear about the rules so they will know when they are broken. Defining some of the more ambiguous areas regarding touch may be an outcome of using the curriculum. Clear definitions, whenever possible, provide safety for all persons in out-of-home care. As types of communication and touch will be a subject of study, the facility will want to examine its guidelines, both overt and covert, about communication, touching, and boundaries.

GROUP MEMBERS

Child Participants

This curriculum can be given to children and adolescents. It is fruitful to have children in the same cottage participate together with the clinicians and caregivers who work with them. This increases generalization of the goals of the curriculum as the caregivers can reinforce the learning goals in the milieu. The material in the curriculum can be used in the cottage following the group, thereby bringing greater learning and more generalization of the prevention material.

Adult Participants

Because out-of-home facilities may have people working in them who themselves can be helped by instruction in healthy emotional, physical, and sexual boundaries, the exercises can be beneficial to the adults and children alike. Social work/clinical staff and cottage caregivers are important group members. The cottage supervisor may also want to participate. As many caregivers as possible should be involved in the exercises. The hope is that all of the caregivers who work in a child's cottage will be able to participate in at least some of the exercises. The group may need to be held at different times so that caregivers from all shifts can attend.

This curriculum attempts to bring a further understanding between the caregivers and the children. A major issue with many children in out-of-home care is that they do not feel connected to anyone and, therefore, have little reason to have a positive attitude toward the other children and adults. Some children in out-of-home care feel little or no connection to anyone. Children move from the stage of following directions because of punishment, to following directions because they want to please someone, through emotional attachments. If children do not feel that people care about them, or they do not care about others, the only thing operating in the environment to control behavior is the reinforcement system. Knowing more about each other and becoming more sensitive to the others' boundaries, feelings, and needs can assist children and caregivers to feel a greater connection. Caregivers who have participated in the curriculum say that they have a totally different view of the children after listening to them in the groups. More of the cares and worries of the children emerge instead of the anger and aggression which may be more evident in the cottage. In some facilities, line staff or the immediate caregivers mainly deal with the children at a behavioral level; this curriculum allows the caregivers the opportunity to "hear" the children.

GROUP LEADERS AND COFACILITATORS

Because of clinicians training in group process and group therapy, they are generally selected as the designated leaders and have the primary responsibility for making the curriculum happen. The point person assumes a leadership role and makes sure all materials required for the exercise are available, prepares the caregivers by reviewing with them the material for the upcoming group, and assures the group is scheduled and that the caregivers participate in the groups.

While the point person is the designated leader, it is most helpful to have the caregivers in the group act as cofacilitators. As a cofacilitator, caregivers participate actively in the exercises by giving examples, fostering dialog, bringing up issues that relate to the children's behaviors in the milieu, and talking about how the material being discussed can be used to change the milieu. Cofacilitators may start and guide some of the exercises. The caregivers may want to take turns having primary responsibility for preparing the sessions.

The curriculum is not meant for the line staff to do with the children without other levels of the facility staff involved. Since children may raise bothersome or possibly abusive behaviors, attitudes, or feelings by caregivers, it is most helpful to have adults with different responsibilities to work through the issues with the caregiver and child. If only one caregiver or one line staff were present, and the children wanted to talk about the way line staff touch or restrain children in the cottage, the caregiver or line staff may never make this information known to supervisors, in an effort to protect themselves. It is extremely detrimental for children in out-of-home care to take the initiative to talk about feeling hurt and then have nothing happen or for vindictive behavior to occur.

It is important that there be the best meshing of the clinicians and cottage caregivers as possible in the group work. In some placements there is an undercurrent of antagonism between the clinicians and the cottage caregivers. This may be related to their different roles with the children and can often be felt by the children. Clinicians sometimes think the caregivers are too harsh, nonempathic, robotic, and punitive with the children. Cottage caregivers may think the clinicians: are too wishy-washy; let the children get too wild and then dump them on the caregivers; think they are superior and talk (stupid) psychobabble. (This takes different forms in different facilities.)

Facilities may recreate the dynamics of the children's home by having divisions and alliances and suballiances, with the children caught in the middle and used as pawns. Some children will feel responsible for the disagreements. This is highly contraindicated. Working together in the group, sharing the leadership role, acting as cofacilitators, and taking turns managing the children's behavioral system (see below) can help to break down these barriers. Each of the team who work with the children must respect the others' work.

The line staff or immediate caregivers should not be used solely as the behavior managers. In many facilities, the line staff have much better control over the children than the clinicians do and are used in group for the purpose of behavior management. This is not the intent of this curriculum. It is very central to the curriculum that all adults participate in the dialog of all of the exercises. Behavior management can be rotated between the adults present. See the section on Behavior Management in the Group below.

Because each session is different and does not necessarily build on a previous session, cofacilitators can change so that as many of the caregivers will be in groups as possible. It is recommended that the designated leader, a clinician, be consistent throughout the entire curriculum.

The style of the cofacilitators is important. They should be very positive, open, reassuring, and confident in the children's ability to enjoy and learn from the exercises.

All caregivers should get an opportunity to be in as many groups as possible. The more caregivers know about the curriculum and its language and teaching, the better the translation into the cottage life.

IMPARTING PERSONAL INFORMATION TO THE CHILDREN

Many out-of-home placements have a policy regarding caregivers disclosing personal information to the children with whom they work. This is often tricky. The material in the curriculum may encourage personal disclosure by caregivers due to its emphasis on touch, communication, boundaries, and abuse. In facilities which do not have a policy, caregivers will decide for themselves. In general, revealing past trauma is not helpful to children as it is their trauma which is important to heal. They must not feel that they need to help the adults who are there to help them. Some children may feel their abuse is not as serious as what happened to a caregiver or may feel competitive with the caregiver.

Caregivers who believe that children will feel better if they know that others have been abused and later flourished, can use books, movies, or magazines for examples of this phenomenon. The children's pain is generally not alleviated by knowing the background or stresses of the caregivers. All energy is best focused on the children's problems.

SUPERVISION

It is important that the caregivers working together in the group get the opportunity to talk outside the group. During this time each adult can: discuss his or her experience in the group, indicate if they need help in knowing how to best participate in the group, and let others know if they feel cut off or uncomfortable in the group, etc. It is best if the adults can meet fairly soon after the group so the information and feelings are still fresh.

This meeting outside the group can be at the same time the planning occurs for the next group, or the planning session can be in closer proximity to the beginning of the next group.

If caregivers feel threatened by the curriculum in any way, their concerns should be addressed. It may occur that caregivers with significant problems in the areas addressed by the curriculum may be obstructive to its implementation.

FEEDBACK TO ALL CAREGIVERS WHO WORK WITH THE CHILDREN IN EACH GROUP

If the groups are made up of children in the same cottage, an update can be given at the weekly staff meeting. Caregivers in that week's group can discuss their experience. The content of the group can be discussed briefly. The best learning is when the group material is generalized into the milieu. Concepts and vocabulary learned in the group can be utilized in the cottage to help the children connect the learning to real life. All caregivers should be aware of the empathy and generalization points. Some cottages may want to add these points to the cottage reinforcement system while the curriculum is being used. (See "How to Use the Behavior Chart" in Appendix B for an explanation of the empathy and generalization points.)

Any outstanding material that occurs during a group that is pertinent to a particular child or the cottage can be logged in the book used for the purpose of ongoing information exchange between shifts.

LENGTH OF GROUP MEETINGS

The length of group meetings, the amount to be covered in each session, the language, and depth of understanding expected will be different depending on the age, developmental level, and cognitive level of the children and adolescents.

Each group period will be at least 45 minutes to an hour for latency-aged children. Older children may be able to manage 60 to 75 minutes. Adolescents may spend 75 to 90 minutes.

Some groups of children will be able to complete a session in one group meeting period. Some groups will require two group periods. Some of the sessions have many facets to them. Repetition is very helpful. Since there is ample time to work with children in out-of-home care, there is no need to move quickly through the material. If a session is to be worked on in a second or additional group meeting time, ask the children to review the general thrust of the previous session. If written material was developed in the previous session, bring it as visual cues to help the children remember the previous week's content.

GROUP SIZE

The size of the group will depend on the facility, the type of children, and how the groups are formed. If all the children in a cottage are to be in the same group, the size of the cottage will dictate the number of children. It is inadvisable to have more than seven or eight children as there is not enough time for each child to speak. There can be many adults. There will be the clinician or the point person and other caregivers from the cottage. Three or four (or more) adults is fine. It is best not to have more adults than children.

BEHAVIOR MANAGEMENT IN THE GROUP

The focus of the group should not be behavior management. When the groups are formed this can be taken into account. The mix of children in a group is always important. If it is possible that the children's behavior will be a problem, a behavioral system can be devised for use in the group. The adults can choose to institute it as the group begins or bring it in, if needed.

All adults in the group can participate in managing the children's behavior. In some instances the cottage line staff are used as the "behavior enforcers" or "police" in groups. This continues to put them in a regulatory function and decreases their ability to be empathic and sensitive to the children. When a behavior system is used, the person in charge of marking down the points can rotate between the adults–with each adult taking a different session. All adults will help the children contain their behavior, yet only one adult keeps the chart.

Behavior charts and a suggestion of how to use it are included in Appendix B. If it is too different from what the children are used to, something akin to this is useful. It is helpful to have points for empathy and generalization. The empathy points are received when a child responds at a feeling level to what another child has said. The generalization points encourage the children to take what they have learned and apply it outside of group. The children can tell the adults during the group how they used something and receive points on that day's chart. If it appears that the children are making up occasions in order to falsely receive points, let them know, in an encouraging manner, that you will talk to the people involved. Since cottage caregivers will be in the group, children can ask them to help remember to tell about pertinent incidents during the week in group. If the caregiver will not be in group, a caregiver who will be in group can be told. In this way the children are aware that the caregivers are helping them and proud that the children are learning and using the material.

STRUCTURING THE GROUP TIME

If possible, a nice way to start group is to have a snack and talk about examples of things that happened during the week which relate to what has been learned in group. In the beginning, caregivers can bring up examples that arose during the week until the children learn to engage in this part of the group. Children are given points on the behavior chart for each example they can discuss which relates group learning to occurrences in the milieu.

Even if there is no snack, this discussion can still be the first part of group.

The structured exercise is then completed. After the structured exercise, homework is explained, if it is to be given.

At the end of the group, the chart is completed (see Appendix B) and group is over. As the children leave group, encourage them to use the material outside the group and to come with examples so they can get points on the behavior chart in the upcoming week.

GROUP PROCESS

Remember to encourage discussion between the whole group—not from each child to an adult. This is like having individual sessions in a group setting. The children can talk to each other or to any of the adults. The adults may want to ask other adults questions. The discussion can be free flowing and fun. Unless necessary for behavior management, children need not raise their hands. This helps the children learn to take turns and listen to others. When children have to raise their hands they are generally not listening but restlessly waving their arms. When they must wait for the other child to finish they have to listen, at least to some extent. Encourage the children to ask *each other* questions. This helps them listen attentively to what the other child has said. Ask the children questions about what another child said to alert them to listen to what everyone says. Remind the children about the empathy points; this encourages the children to listen to one another.

The pace should be fast and fun. Caregivers can be active participants in the role plays and every other aspect of the group.

It is important to listen carefully to what the children are saying in the group. If there are transgressions by the caregivers, children, or anyone else they must be attended to right away. This is discussed in the next section.

ALLEGATIONS OF ABUSE OR MISUSE

If a child talks about minor interactions with the caregivers which he or she does not like, this can be handled in the group. If a child is speaking specifically about a caregiver who is not in the group, the discussion can be made more general to interactions with caregivers or it can be suggested that an adult assist the child to discuss the concern with the particular caregiver of concern after group. It is not helpful to discuss at any length the behavior of a caregiver who is not present. This will cause caregiver's concern that when they are not in group, they will be discussed.

If a child makes an allegation of abuse by an adult who is present in the group, this must be handled carefully. The facility may want to decide how they want a situation such as this handled. Generally, it would be recommended that the assertion is noted and an agreement is made to discuss the situation immediately after group. While some background information may need to be determined, it is the work of child protective services to investigate child abuse. Lengthy discussion of abuse allegations in the group will not be useful to the investigation nor to the other children in the group nor to the feelings of the person who is being accused.

If an allegation of abuse is made about a person who is not in the group, an agreement can be made to discuss this immediately after group. It is important that this discussion be immediate. It will not be helpful to the child to feel that when they say abuse happens there is not immediate follow-up. This may have happened in their own home. It will also be important to protect the child from any possible retribution or threat. If the allegation is not true it will be important to clear it up.

In several places in the curriculum there are strong warnings about alleging abuse or misuse which did not occur. When children are being taught their rights, especially children who have been previously maltreated and are alone, there may be a need to caution them about the damage which can be done to an individual if a false allegation is made. This curriculum has been done with many children and no false allegations have been made, but reminding them will still serve its purpose.

KEEPING THE MATERIAL FROM EACH SESSION

All of the materials developed in each of the sessions should be saved. Some exercises use work developed in previous groups. Also, at the end of all of the sessions, it is very useful to review the work done during the course of the curriculum. The children can be asked which parts they liked and which parts they didn't like. They can remember funny or sad times. This further enhances and emphasizes the content and reinforces learning.

INDIVIDUAL, FAMILY SESSIONS, AND MULTIFAMILY GROUPS

Clinicians who provide individual therapy for the children in the groups may want to use the exercises in the individual sessions to reinforce the learning and help the child with the intrapsychic struggles related to the material.

It is strongly encouraged that the sessions on "Prevention of Sexual Misuse or Abuse" be done in family sessions prior to the child returning home. In fact, all of the exercises are very suitable for family sessions of any abused child who will be returning home.

Some facilities provide reunification services to the children and families with whom they work. The whole curriculum can be used with families or with many families together. As there is a great deal of abuse which occurs in the family context and may not have been resolved, this material will assist to prevent further emotional, physical, or sexual abuse.

THE CURRICULUM AND THERAPY

The curriculum does not replace therapy for children who have been abused. It does have a very palliative effect on children and is therapeutic. Many children who have been through the curriculum's exercises have revealed a great deal which was unknown by the caregivers and clinicians to its use. The group format and the supportive nature of the exercises appears to encourage the children to talk about prior abuse, fears, and disappointments. The curriculum encourages children to find solutions to their dilemmas. This, in turn, increases their sense of self-efficacy.

ISSUES MAY ARISE THAT WILL NEED INTERVENTION

Some residential facilities have more problems than others with the issues that will be raised in this curriculum. It is important for an institution to realize that if problems in communication, physical contact, or sexual behavior arise during the implementation of the curriculum, the issues will need to be addressed head on.

This curriculum may surface children who are being emotionally, physically, or sexually abusive to other children. If children are being abusive, their treatment plans will need to be revised to meet their needs, or, if not possible due to caregiver's expertise, training, and/or the physical plant, a transfer will need to be made to another facility where the abusive behavior can be treated without other children being hurt.

Issues that arise should be used as an opportunity for growth. Most children in residential settings have been victimized in their homes. When issues surface that need modifying and the children can see action taken, it has an enormously beneficial effect. Many victimized children internalize a sense of helplessness and hopelessness in their homes which can be furthered by being in an "institution" with many, many different caregivers a week upon whom the children feel they can have little impact. Unfortunately some facilities do not respond to children who complain. Staff continue to be overly punitive in the name of behavior management. This increases the despair of children and mimics their home environment from which they were removed because the adults were meeting their own needs instead of caring for the children. This curriculum provides the forum for communication between caregivers and children as the children grow and develop in their self-understanding.

If caregivers are deficient in their interactions with the children, this will need to be rectified. Some behaviors may surface that will require an incident report, a child abuse report, or increased training. It is important to realize that issues that surface may indicate underlying problems. One of the benefits of the curriculum is that it gives the children and caregivers a vehicle to express themselves.

ORDERING SUPPLEMENTARY MATERIALS

Books published by Channing L. Bete titled *As Boys Grow Up, As Girls Grow Up,* and *As You Grow Up* can be ordered from: Scriptographic Booklets Channing Bete Co. Inc. South Deerfield, MA 01373. The toll-free number is 1-800-499-6464. These books are used in Exercise Four, Chapter 6.

Other books also sold by Channing L. Bete that may be helpful are:

- *Abstinence–Saying "No" to Sex*
- *Talking to Adolescents About Sex*
- *Making Responsible Choices About Sex*
- *What Everyone Should Know About STDs*
- *What Everyone Should Know About the Sexual Abuse of Children*

- *About Sex and Alcohol*
- *What You Should Know About Teenage Pregnancy*

The game *Let's Talk About Touching* is very useful in helping the children talk about the prevention rules and answer questions about touching problems between children and between children and grownups. The game is an optional part of the curriculum. See Chapter Four, Exercise Two. To order send $19.00 for North America, $23.00 airmail overseas, or $20.00 surface overseas to cover shipping and handling. The game will be sent within three weeks. Order from: Toni Cavanagh Johnson, PhD, 1101 Fremont Ave. Suite 101, South Pasadena, CA 91011.

Chapter 2

Exploring Communication

OBJECTIVES

- To understand the differences between comforting and soothing communication, taking care of communication, expressing a need, neutral communication, no communication, confusing communications, and harmful and hurtful communications.
- To understand these types of communication between children, from adults to children, and from children to adults.
- To explore how tone, choice of words, and body posture affect communication.
- To relate all concepts to communication in out-of-home care.
- To relate the concept of verbal communication to emotional abuse and neglect.
- To help children learn how to communicate their needs, ask others to stop speaking to them in hurtful ways, and to know to whom to go for help if people continue to speak to them negatively.
- To learn how to get positive needs met.
- To sensitize all adults in out-of-home care to how and what they communicate to children in their care.
- To encourage all adults in out-of-home care to be aware that *everything* they say to the child contributes to or diminishes the child's sense of self.

RATIONALE AND PURPOSE

Children in residential care have generally experienced physical, sexual, or emotional abuse, neglect, and/or abandonment.

This exercise is to help the children understand the different types of communications they receive and send that contribute to a feeling of discomfort or lead to misuse or abuse.

As a consequence of what has been done and said to them and what they have witnessed, these children often have severe difficulties in communicating effectively. They do not know how to seek nurturance or defend against hurt. Many only know how to be hurtful with their communications, mimicking what has been done to them.

The purpose of this exercise is to make communication conscious to all who participate. There is far too much said that is potentially damaging between all sectors in out-of-home care. The exercises will go beyond the words to the facial expressions, voice tones, and body language.

As the continuum is worked on, communications between children, between parents and children, and between out-of-home care staff and children will all come under scrutiny. Open and frank discussion encourages children to understand their rights and provides a forum for discussion. A problem-solving discussion about ongoing communication problems will teach positive skills for resolving conflict. The children should understand their rights regarding how they are spoken to and their responsibility related to speaking to others.

EXERCISE ONE:
A CONTINUUM OF COMMUNICATION I

Materials:

Newsprint and stand
Wide Markers

1. Explain to the children that, "There are many different things people say to each other and they often use their body to commu-

nicate also. Some things are said in a nice voice and the person's body looks gentle. It is as important to pay attention to what is said as how it is said and the person's body language. Overall, this is called communication. In the next exercises we are going to focus on communication between people in your home, here, and any other place you may have lived. While we are doing this exercise pay lots of attention to how we communicate with each other in this group and how everyone communicates with one another in the cottage. This will come in handy when we are looking for examples. This week we are going to focus on what is said. Next week we will pay attention to the body language."

2. Draw a line on the newsprint. Put the following from left to right on top of the line: "comforting and soothing," "taking care of," "expressing a need," "neutral," "no communication," "confusing," and "harmful and hurtful." For younger children you may want to use fewer categories. They may want different categories. Some groups may want "defensive" or "rejecting." Let them have whatever fits best. Leaders will assure that the objectives of the exercise are handled by the categories which are developed. If they are not, encourage the children to make additions.

3. Ask the children to come up with examples of communications that fit in each of the categories. In this exercise focus on the verbal message, i.e., the words said. Examples are:

- *Comforting and soothing*—"I think you will make the team." "I have felt that way before and I got over it." "Your mother will come back." "She was just being mean she really cares about you."
- *Taking care of*—"I'll take care of you." "When you feel really lousy, call me." "Can I get you something?" "I'll be here for you." "Do you want me to read to you?"
- *Expressing a need*—"I'm sad." "Get out of here." "I'm scared." "I need my space." "I am lonely."

- *Neutral*–Communications about a movie, directions to the park, or the outline of the day's activities, etc.
- *No communication*–Name-calling arguments in which no one is listening and is only trying to hurt the other person. Heated discussions in which one person attacks and the other is defensive. A child who refuses to say anything to anyone. An absence of positive reinforcement. No calls from home. The person refuses to talk when asked questions.
- *Confusing*–"You are ungrateful, you should like it here." "It's all your fault you are there." (Parent to child in residential facility due to abuse in home.)
- *Harmful and hurtful*–"Get out of my face." "You jerk." "You are the reason I abandoned you." "Your breath is kicking like Van Damme."

The communications can be from anyone. The adults should encourage the children to come up with real examples from their parents, in the facility, or in previous placements. If some communication occurs during the exercise that would be a good example, use it. Using examples that are well understood because they just happened is often the most effective way for the children to learn.

4. After there are many examples, ask the children to look at them and associate feelings and thoughts with different types of communications.

- Can feelings or thoughts you get when things are said to you help you figure out which category the message is in?
- How do you feel when you get hurtful messages? Think of one and tell what you felt and what you wanted to do.
- Are there lots of different feelings with the same type of messages?
- How do people feel who say hurtful things to others?
- Are there different feelings you get from different staff even if they are telling you the same thing?

- What kinds of things do people say to give children safe feelings, scared feelings, sexual feelings, etc.?
- Have you ever thought someone was being mean to you by what they said and they really didn't mean to?

5. It can be helpful to look at the difference between what someone means to communicate and what the person who hears it understands, or feels, about the communication. For instance, "You are ungrateful, you should like it here" could be a *confusing* message coming out of a staff person's mouth but a child could receive it as *harmful and hurtful*. Someone simply *expressing a need* to be alone, "Leave me alone" or "Get out" could be perceived as *harmful and hurtful* to the person hearing it. The person receiving that message may not take into account how the other person feels at the moment. They may feel that no one likes them or wants to be around them.

6. Save the continuum and bring to the next session.

EXERCISE TWO:
A CONTINUUM OF COMMUNICATION II

Materials:

Newsprint and stand
Wide Markers
The continuum sheets from previous session
Each category of the continuum written on approximately 6-inch tall poster board

1. The focus of this session is to have the children pay attention to the voice tone, voice quality, facial movements, gestures, and body posture of the person speaking to them as well as the words being said. The children should also pay attention to their own communications, body posture, and voice tone. Children

often accept confusing, harmful, or hurtful messages as well as give them. This exercise is to heighten their awareness about negative communications. Asking people to stop talking to them in negative ways and understanding emotional abuse are also part of this session.

2. Ask the children to remember the continuum. If they cannot remember some of the parts let them guess for a while. Give them examples of the types of communication they are forgetting. Then show them the signs you have made out of poster board.

3. Ask for a volunteer to put the cards in order along the wall of a room.

Alternative A

4. Ask for a volunteer to stand in front of the group and try to show one of the types of communication using only facial expressions. Before the child goes up in front of the group, he or she should whisper to an adult the type of communication to be performed. In this way the child cannot change based on what the group guesses. Each child should have an opportunity. Try to have the children cover each of the communication types. Staff should join in. This is a nice way to see how the children can read the body language of each other and the staff.

After facial expressions have been completed, add the body gestures (hands, head, arms), posture, and body movement.

Encourage the children to understand their own body language. It can be fun for the children to study their own body stances when they are communicating different feelings. Highlight the importance of body language in communication. A person's body language alone can get someone mad at them.

5. Next explore voice tone, pitch, loudness, and quality. Ask the children to give examples combining the voice and the body language. Demonstrate the additive quality of insult or pleasure

when voice and body are combined with the content of the communication.

Alternative B

4. Ask children if they can imagine any things that are said that would change meaning depending on the tone of voice, the body posture, the facial movements, or gestures of the person. Ask them to come up with examples of things being said with one voice tone that feels good to them and the exact same thing being said that makes them feel unhappy. Examples from the continuum of the previous session can be used or the examples given below can be used. Ask the children to demonstrate the different examples. As they give the different examples, ask which categories on the continuum the examples fit.

Have a good time with this exercise while assuring that the children become aware of what they do with their communications and also what is done to them. Encourage the children to understand their own body language. It can be fun for the children to study their own body stances when they are communicating different feelings. Highlight the importance of body language in communication. A person's body language alone can get someone mad at them.

Examples:

- Come here, I want to hug you.
- Get out of here.
- I'm sad.
- My sister is in Arizona. I miss her when she is not here.
- I hate you.
- I'm hungry.
- I always love you but sometimes you act terrible and I feel like I hate you.
- It is time for a bath.

- You are acting like a brat.
- Where were you?
- Take the trash out.
- It's nice to be with you.
- Why do you always do that?
- Here's dinner.
- Are you hungry?
- You should never have been born.
- You can be my special friend.
- I saw a dog that was hurt.
- No, there is no time to do that now.
- It doesn't matter if your mother gets mad; who cares about her?
- I know you don't want to do this, but I'll hurt you if you don't.
- I'll tell on you if you don't do what I want.
- I'll let you do what you want if you won't tell your mother about our game.
- You are stupid if you think you can get away with that.
- Get out of my room, you idiot.
- I feel happy today.
- You are so stupid; you do everything wrong.
- I feel better when I am with you.
- I'm scared; what should I do?
- We cannot seem to agree.
- You look like your father.
- You act like your mother.
- Stop doing that.
- No, you can't go out to play.

5. If it does not happen spontaneously, the leaders should point out examples of emotionally hurtful messages and the impact on the person. Leaders can stress the content that is hurtful or abusive and the voice tone and physical postures that can make any

statement hurtful regardless of the content. The children should be aware of how they are emotionally hurtful or abusive to one another and to staff, and how adults have been emotionally hurtful or abusive to them.

EXERCISE THREE:
HARMFUL AND HURTFUL COMMUNICATIONS I

Materials:

Newsprint and stand
Wide Markers
The continuum sheets from previous session
Each category of the continuum written on approximately 6-inch tall poster board
Worksheet #1 in Appendix C

1. Ask the children to recall the categories on the continuum. Give high praise for children who can remember them.

2. Hang the previous continuum, which has examples, where it can be seen. Look at examples of harmful and hurtful communications. If more are needed, ask for more examples. Use these as the basis for the grid described in the next step.

3. On a clean sheet draw a grid. On the top of the left hand column put "Harmful or Hurtful Messages." (See Figure 2.1.) On the top of the right hand column put "Saying It Like It Is Without Hurting." Encourage the children and the staff to work on ways of getting the point across but not devastating the other person. Children and staff should realize that this type of communication allows the recipient to maintain a positive sense of self. Self-esteem is the foundation of healthy people.

FIGURE 2.1

Harmful or Hurtful Messages	Saying It Like It Is Without Hurting
"You idiot! I don't want you on my team."	"I'm not going to pick you because we fight a lot."
"I hate him; he looks like a geek."	"We don't get along."
"You little turd."	"I get really annoyed with the way you _____."
"You are such a slob."	"It makes me upset when you are so messy."
"Get the hell out of my way, you _____."	"Please move right now."
"You should never have been born."	"I'm furious at you."
"You are so stupid; you do every-thing wrong."	"Please slow down and try harder."

Some caregivers may verge on saying hurtful things to children. This is a good opportunity for everyone to learn positive styles of communication. If this is brought up, put some of these things in the grid and problem solve how caregivers can say them without being hurtful.

4. Generally there is an interaction between the speaker and person spoken to. In the second part of this exercise, point out through role plays the interaction effect on communications. For instance, a staff person may start shouting because a child will not obey the directions. A child may not see the effect of their behavior on the staff person. The body signals given by staff or children or what is said may have the effect of bringing forth a response from the other person. Using light humor, not mockery, as a vehicle, try to have each person act out how he or she "gives an attitude." Ask others to say what they feel like doing when they get an attitude. Ask the person what causes them to "give an attitude."

5. Encourage the children and staff to be very aware of their surroundings during the coming week and bring back to the group next week examples of harmful or hurtful communica-

tions. If the children are capable of successfully completing home-work sheets, give them copies of Worksheet #1 from Appendix C. They can get a point for each example they come up with if they return the sheet at the next session. If not, ask them to remember some examples and ask the staff to cue them about this one day before the next group.

Some of the children may want to do a different assignment. Children are to observe staff, parents, other children, and primar-ily themselves to learn how feelings are communicated through the body. Feelings could be happiness, sadness, deep depression, anger, disappointment, curiosity, or an attitude, etc.

Children are to observe carefully and be prepared to do a mime of three people. If other group members can guess the people being mimed, each will get points for generalization. Children should not be disrespectful or hurtful to the people they are imitating. Children must include at least two ways in which they use their bodies when "feeling" strongly. Imitating them-selves can be combined with imitating others so that it is good fun to determine who is being imitated feeling what feeling.

Let the children know that each example brought back to the group will be awarded a point on the behavior management chart under "An Example from Real Life of Something You Learned in Group."

EXERCISE FOUR:
HARMFUL AND HURTFUL COMMUNICATIONS II

Materials:

Newsprint and stand
Wide Markers
Worksheet #2 in Appendix C

1. On a clean sheet draw a grid. On the top of the left hand column write "Harmful and Hurtful Talk." On the top of the

middle column write "Saying It Like It Is Without Attacking and Hurting." On the top of the far column write "Responding to Harmful and Hurtful Talk." (See Figure 2.2.) Ask for examples for the first column. Then encourage the children and the staff to work on ways of getting the point across without devastating the other person. Children and staff should realize that this type of communication allows the recipient to maintain a positive sense of self and not feel angry or defensive.

FIGURE 2.2

Harmful and Hurtful (Attacking) Talk	Saying It Like It Is Without Attacking and Hurting	Responding to Harmful and Hurtful Talk
"Your breath is kicking like Van Damme."	"Could you please go brush your teeth?"	"Please stop talking to me like that."
"You are such a slob."	"It makes me upset when you are so messy."	"You hurt my feelings when you talk to me that way."
"**Get** in your room **right now**." (yelling)	"Please go to your room." (not yelling) "Ladies, please go to your room."	"Why are you yelling? I don't feel like doing what you want when you yell at me."

Since children in their abusive or neglectful homes and sometimes in out-of-home care, in school, and in the community are spoken to in harmful and hurtful ways, the last column is reserved for learning how to respond to communications that feel bad to the recipient. Practice with the children how to tell someone that they don't like the way they are talking to them. Encourage the children to come up with different ways of doing this. Using the examples from the first column, ask the children to fill in the third column. Examples are:

• You hurt my feelings when you talk to me that way.
• Please stop talking to me like that.

- I get scared when you talk like that.
- Why are you yelling?
- You are scaring me.
- When you stand like that I think you are going to hurt me.

2. Children should be aware that harmful and hurtful messages from children or adults are not all right. When adults who care for them speak in harmful and hurtful ways this is called emotional abuse. Children should be helped to know what they should do to get help to stop this from happening. Remind the children that if they feel uncomfortable they should speak to the person who is making them feel this way or they should go to an adult they trust and tell them. It may be necessary for an adult to help children in out-of-home care with another adult in the facility or with their parents.

3. Give the children copies of Worksheet #2 from Appendix C. They can get a point for each example they come up with if they return the sheet at the next session.

4. If it seems like it would be useful, ask the group if they want to have someone type up the grid, or they could hand write it. Someone in the group can draw a cover, come up with a catchy name and distribute it to other staff and children. The pamphlet can explain to other people about communication. The children may want to include something about emotional abuse and what to do about it.

5. This exercise can be done at a later time in individual therapy or in a family session(s).

6. Reinforce all participants to be aware of the messages they send with their voice, facial expressions, and body posture.

Chapter 3

Exploring Touch

OBJECTIVES

- To understand the differences between comforting and soothing touch, caretaking touch, accidental or neutral touch, no touch, confusing touch, harmful and hurtful touch, and violent touch.
- To understand different types of touch between children, adult to child, child to adult, and between people and animals.
- To relate the concept of touch and physical or sexual abuse and neglect.
- To relate the concepts of different types of touch to life in out-of-home care.
- To help children use their feelings as guideposts for knowing different types of touch.
- To bring up the idea of feelings and thoughts children may have that would lead them to want to touch another child or an adult.
- To know the rules about touch in the facility including physical restraints if the child is out of control.
- To understand children's rights related to touch. To encourage children to tell when they are being touched in a confusing, harmful and hurtful, or violent way.
- To assure children know to whom to report suspected abuse.
- To sensitize children regarding the seriousness of making abuse allegations.
- To sensitize child care providers to all of the above concepts and to help them understand the children's perspective.

RATIONALE AND PURPOSE

Children in residential care have generally experienced physical, sexual, or emotional abuse, neglect, and/or abandonment. They also may have observed violence at close range. As a consequence of what has been done to them and what they have witnessed, these children often have difficulties in the area of touch.

This exercise uses a continuum to help children understand the different types of touches. Some children only think of being hit or not hit, sexually abused or not, i.e., touch or no touch, good touch, bad touch. An unfortunate effect of some prevention programs is an emphasis on "bad touch." It is essential that children connect positive feelings and behaviors to touch. For many children negativity has been overly associated with sexuality. Children with sexual behavior problems will spontaneously associate touching with negative sex. "Touching will lead to bad things." It is very important that children see the whole range of touch and that sex not be associated with only negative outcomes. Sexual curiosity must not be forgotten. There is a whole range of touching and looking that is very normative in children. Sexuality and touching *must not* be associated with fear, shame, or guilt for children. This will be a strong impediment to their developing sexuality.

Touch ranges from healthy to hurtful, from nurturing to damaging. A continuum of touch includes: comforting and soothing touch, taking care of touch, playful touch, accidental or neutral touch, no touch, confusing touch, harmful and hurtful touch, and violent touch. When children can differentiate between types of touch, they have a better understanding of the kind of touch they have received and what they want to receive. Children can be aware of the feelings they get from the range of touching. Children should be helped to understand that they can question what is happening to them. They should know their rights regarding who touches them and how.

Touching has different connotations in different cultures. While some cultures hug and kiss only within the family, others may extend this to friends and friends of friends. The distance people stand from one another, the type of handshakes, the type of hug, and the kind of kiss can have different meanings in different cultures. Some cultures do very little touching, some a great deal. Be sensitive to cultural differences when exploring this topic.

Each facility should have guidelines for the staff regarding physical contact with the children. Do staff hug the children? What types of hugs? Do they give back rubs? Etc.

Because of the level of behavioral difficulty in children in out-of-home care some children will need to be restrained. The rules regarding restraints, when they are used and who can do them, should be thoroughly explained to the children.

While there are physical restraints at RTCs, the children need to know that this is under their control. If a child does not get out of control, physical restraint will not be used. During these restraints staff should try to be careful that there is no contact, except perhaps accidental, with the children's genitals. If contact with the genitals does occur, it may be advisable for the staff person to note this to the child and state that it was by accident. Children who have been physically and sexually abused can misperceive staff intentions during restraints. Some children seek out restraints for the physical contact. Some children experience PTSD (post-traumatic stress disorder) symptoms during restraints. This is a very difficult area for staff and needs constant attention and supervision.

When the issue of touch from caregivers to children or children to caregiver is discussed, the loss of parental touch can be explored. This may lead to a discussion of the greater safety the children feel in out-of-home care and their parents' need to learn not to hit. It may also lead to a discussion of certain staff persons' touches or those of certain children toward staff which need modification.

Sexual touch between children is a very problematic issue in out-of-home care. Preventing abuse from child-to-child is a focus of this curriculum. Yet, it is also important to remember that if children were not in out-of-home care, they would very likely be engaging in sexual exploration with other children. This is a healthy interest in children. Because there is such high supervision of children, the natural exploration and talk children generally engage in about sex is curtailed. This tends to increase its salience. Caregivers will be advised not to sexualize or overly identify sexual behaviors in children in their care. While they need to protect children from abuse, they do not need to protect them from normal curiosity or shame them for sexual interest. Generally in out-of-home care there are so many children with problems that all natural curiosity is stifled for fear it will get out of control. Protection of the children is essential. But beware not to find sexual contact where it isn't. Staff may be overly sensitive to children sitting close to one another to read a book, roughhousing or playing football, or other contact sports. Children need to have body contact and know that it is not wrong. If sexual behaviors between consenting teenagers occur, they can be told that this type of behavior may be acceptable outside the facility but while the children live in out-of-home care, it is not allowed. This is an attempt to normalize sexual behavior between consenting teenagers so they do not get the idea that all sex needs to be sneaked, is bad, or unacceptable.

Many children in out-of-home care have observed abusive interactions including battering in their homes. The exercises in this module can be used in family meetings. Prevention exercises provided in the family are very beneficial. Exercises can help sensitize parents to preventing abuse to their children.

GENERAL INSTRUCTIONS

This module can be done in three or more sessions. In the first session, the continuum is drawn and children are asked to fill in different types of touch. While examples are sought for each category, the emphasis in this first session is directed to comforting and soothing touch, caretaking touch, accidental or neutral touch, and no touch. The second session will focus on the confusing touch, harmful and hurtful touch, and violent touch. In some cases, leaders may want to have more sessions on this material.

The children will often talk about touches from adults to them. In addition, ask the children to find examples for each of the categories of touches between children and from children to adults.

EXERCISE ONE:
A CONTINUUM OF TOUCH I

Materials:

Newsprint and stand
Wide Markers
Each category of continuum written on approximately 6-inch tall
   poster board

1. Write the categories on the newsprint. If the children decide on other categories this is fine, if the goals of the exercises are met.

2. Ask the children to begin to describe different touches they have experienced which fit these categories. The therapist can write the children's responses underneath the line so they can be reviewed at the end of the session and in future sessions. Tell the children that they should put examples in each category, but the main emphasis this week is on comforting and soothing touch, taking care of touch, accidental or neutral touch, and no touch.

If the children seem to be giving examples that have no personal significance, ask them about touches from their parents, relatives, teachers, other adults, teenagers or children, and touches they have given to others.

3. If the children are having trouble coming up with types of touch, the following can be used as examples. Ask the children in which categories these examples would fit best. Examples are: hot hands (the game); tag; football; sparring; reading a book with someone; combing or cutting hair; applying a bandage or a brace; a pat on the back or shoulder; tussle of the child's hair; hugs; side-ways hug; shaking hands; putting medicine on a child's genitals; a rectal exam; a frontal hug; masturbation; foot massage; doctor's examination; pinching; or bumping into someone, etc.

Use examples which occur in group as they are concrete and current.

4. As the children progress, encourage them to explore all types of physical contact. Raise the issue of the absence of touch. In some out-of-home care facilities touch is very restricted. This can have adverse effects on children. In fact, children can be more susceptible to sexual abuse when they hunger for emotional and physical contact.

5. Encourage the children to associate feelings with different touches. Keep the emphasis on the positive or neutral touches. Choose questions which will help the children think about this material. Ask for examples from their own experiences regarding these questions.

- How do children feel when they get the different types of touch?
- Can feelings you get help identify which touch is in which category?
- Can there be lots of different feelings with the same type of touch?
- Does the person who receives the touch feel the same as the person giving the touch? Give an example.
- How do hugs from adults feel?
- Are hugs from other adults a good substitute for hugs from parents and relatives?

- Are there kinds of touch you would like but do not get?
- Are there types of touch you try to get?
- Can you tell by knowing the person what kind of touch they are going to give you?
- If someone is watching you get touched, can they tell what your feelings are about the touch?
- Can someone be trying to give you a comforting touch but it feels bad to you?

6. Discuss the rules in the out-of-home facility about touch.

- Are there rules in the facility about touches between staff and children?
- Are there rules in the facility about touches between children?
- Are the rules reasonable?
- Are they the same as the rules at home?
- Which of the facility rules about touching are broken most often?

7. Save the continuum for use in the next session.

EXERCISE TWO:
A CONTINUUM OF TOUCH II

Materials:

Newsprint and stand
Markers
Each category of the continuum written on approximately 6-inch tall poster board (the length of the poster board will fit the size of the category)

1. Bring back the categories written in large letters on poster board. Ask one or two children to take the categories and line

them up along the wall in the order they think they belong. This will help the children remember the categories as they struggle with remembering the order. The category of "no touch" may be surprising. Some children put this category at the far end of the continuum after harmful and hurtful or violent touch. The categories do not have to stay in the original order if the children do not experience them in that way.

2. Bring back the papers of the continuum with the examples from the previous session. Briefly go over the work done in the last session. If children have other things they want to include, do so. Then talk about the confusing, harmful and hurtful, and violent touch categories. Ask the children to think of examples. (Tell them not to include sexual touches at this time.) If the children seem to be giving examples which have no personal significance, ask them about touches they have received from their parents, relatives, teachers, other adults, teenagers, children, and caregivers. Ask the children to give examples of touches they have given to all different age people which fit in the categories.

3. During the exercise examples of physical abuse and neglect from adults to children and children to children should be raised. If it is not done by the children, the adults should make up examples. Examples of things which have been "read in the newspapers" can be given. Ask if the children know of any other examples.

4. If children bring up concerns about touch by staff members who are present, a discussion about the touching can take place. The children should see that an open discussion can occur and a resolution sought. This will provide a healthy modeling of problem discussion.

If an allegation of abuse is made in group, it is better to agree to discuss this in detail right after group. Assure the child making the assertion that the matter will be discussed immediately after group. As abuse allegations may be misguided, a full and confidential discussion will need to be outside the hearing of the children. Yet, if it turns out that abuse has occurred, the children deserve to know the true facts. Secrets should not be kept, as information this serious may get distorted. Children's fears for their own safety need to be allayed.

If a child refers to behaviors of a staff person not in the group, the leaders should listen carefully to the child and suggest a meeting with that staff person or another resolution satisfactory to the child. Some children are afraid to speak directly to a staff member about these issues. The leaders must assure the child that they will assist in helping the child. Detailed discussions about someone who works in the facility but is not present are not advisable and may lead caregivers to be uneasy with the curriculum.

5. Encourage the children to associate feelings and thoughts with confusing, harmful and hurtful, and violent touches. Use questions such as the following to encourage discussion.

- What kinds of feelings do children get when someone physically hurts them? Is this different than an emotional hurt?
- What kinds of feelings do children get when someone is touching their bodies in a confusing way?
- Sometimes children hurt adults. What types of feelings and thoughts might the adults have?
- Do children sometimes feel like it is their fault if someone hurts them by hitting them too hard?
- Some children seem to want adults to hit them. Is this ever true?
- Some children seem to get out of control so they will get restrained. Why might this be?
- What do children do with these feelings?

6. Children should realize the seriousness of being abused and that anyone who hurts them must be stopped. Reporting abuse should also be stressed. An allegation of abuse should *never* be

made by a child if the child knows it is not true. An untrue allegation should never be made to *hurt or get back at* someone. The damage to a person's reputation can be permanent.

Children should also understand that they may need help to understand if something is abuse. In this case they can ask an adult they trust.

7. This exercise can be reviewed at a later time in individual therapy. Aspects of the exercises in this module are also very useful to do in family therapy. Prevention is very effective with the parents and children together.

EXERCISE THREE:
SEXUAL TOUCH–A CONTINUUM
FROM COMFORTING AND SOOTHING
TO HARMFUL AND HURTFUL AND VIOLENT

Materials:

Newsprint and stand
Wide Markers
Each category of the continuum written on approximately 6-inch
   tall poster board (the length of the poster board will fit the size
   of the category)

1. Ask the children to recall from memory the categories used in the previous two sessions. Write them on the newsprint as they remember them. (For fun, you can have the pile of poster board signs with the names of the categories and hand them each one as they remember it. "Only four more to get; three more; two more; you're almost there.")

2. Generally, children do not remember the categories in order. Ask them to put a number next to the categories to put them in order. Write them out in the order the children agree upon, on the poster board paper. This is to reinforce their learning of the continuum.

3. Then ask where sexual touching comes on the continuum. As they try to place it in one of the categories, help them arrive at the understanding that sexual touching can span all the categories. An example can be kissing. Ask them how many categories kissing could fall in. Another example can be touching the bottom of a person or rubbing another person's leg. Help them to see that even though a part of the body may be considered a sexual part, not all touching is sexual. An example can be kissing from a father to a child or the nursing of an infant or rubbing the leg of a child. Help the children explore all these areas. Encourage them to give examples. If sexual touching has a negative connotation, help the children understand that sex is a natural and healthy aspect of life. (Exercise Two in Chapter 7 brings up these examples in relation to sex offenders grooming children and how a seemingly nonsexual touch can convert into a sexual touch.)

4. Ask them to give examples of touching the private parts for each category. Use the terminology vagina, penis, breasts, anus, testicles, and buttocks (bottom) rather than the more generic "private parts" to assist in diminishing any uneasiness with the proper vocabulary. Look for examples of touch that span all age groups and mixtures of age groups. These touches can be from adult to adult, child to adult, adult to child, child to child, adolescent to child, etc.

5. If it seems to fit in the discussion, broaden the term sexual to mean more than genital or erotic.

Sexual aspects of a person include: their gender identity, that is, do they feel like a boy or a girl; their sexual object choice, that is are they sexually interested in males or females; their genitals; their gender role, that is do they "act like" a boy or a girl; their sexual behavior; their thoughts and feelings regarding sex; ways in which they get pleasure from the stimulation of the genitals, etc. Sexual can refer to hugging and kissing between two people who love each other. Sexual can refer to sexual intercourse through which people express their caring for each other. Sexual can also refer to sexual curiosity, which all children have. Encourage the children to see the full range of sexuality and sexual experience. Emphasize the use of sexual touching to express caring and love.

Ask for lots of examples of children's sexual interest. Ask which category children's sexual curiosity would fall in. Could these be best placed in "playful" or "neutral?"

Allow the opportunity for the children to discuss confusing, harmful and hurtful, or violent sexual touch from child to child. If there are children who have molested children in the group, this will be especially important.

6. The following questions may help the children gain more from this exercise.

- Can a sex offender fool children with touch? Do you think a child might think they were getting a comforting and soothing touch but it really was a sexual touch for the offender?
- In how many categories does the touching of children's genitals fit?
- Do children sometimes feel like it is their fault if someone touches their private parts?
- What do children do with these feelings?
- What kinds of feelings do children get when someone is touching them on their private parts?
- Some children like the body feelings they get when someone touches their private parts. Has this happened to any of you? When that happens does it make it hard to tell the person to stop?
- Sometimes adults want to touch children in a sexual way. What types of feelings and thoughts might make an adult want to touch a child?
- Sometimes children want to touch adults in a sexual way. What types of feelings and thoughts might make a child want to touch an adult?

- Is it more confusing if a child wants to touch your private parts or an adult?
- What kinds of feelings and/or thoughts do children get when they want to touch another child on the private parts?
- Do some children do harmful and hurtful or violent sexual touching to other children?
- Is it possible for a child to do harmful and hurtful sexual touching to an adult?
- Is all touching of private parts between children harmful and hurtful?

Chapter 4

Differentiating
Between Sexual Play
and Sexual Abuse

OBJECTIVES

- To teach children about natural and healthy curiosity and sexual exploration.
- To teach them what is sexually abusive.
- To assist children to discuss their own sexual victimization.
- To assist children to distinguish between sex play and sexual touch which is not okay.
- To assist children to be aware of abusive sexual behavior by themselves and others.
- To portray sex as a healthy part of life.
- To provide sexual abuse prevention information to children.
- To encourage the development of problem-solving skills.
- To assist parents and children to talk together about sexual topics.

RATIONALE AND PURPOSE

In the following exercise, children are asked to think about sexual behaviors and how they would know if a child was being abusive to them. While there are generally no sexual behaviors allowed between children in out-of-home care, the behaviors occur. Generally, not even the most rigorous system of surveillance stops all sexual behavior in out-of-home care. Reiterate the rules of the facility regarding sexual behaviors between children before this exercise. Explain that the exercise is being done in case any children are being abusive in out-of-home care, at their homes, or in the community. If they do not go out of the facility yet, they will need to be aware that other children may try to trick them into sexual behavior which is not in their best interest.

Children with sexual behavior problems need guidelines for their behavior. These children are confused about boundaries, space, sexuality, and relationships among other things. It must not be assumed that the children know right from wrong in these areas. Teaching them in a nonjudgmental and straightforward manner is helpful.

There are many responses that children have to being sexually abused. Some children engage in sexual behaviors beyond what is generally expected. These children may be reenacting their own abuse, acting out their sexual confusion, trying to find caring and comfort, or purposely hurting other people with sex. Whatever the response, there is a great deal of clarification they need about these sexual behaviors. In the second exercise, the game *Let's Talk About Touching* asks many questions for the purpose of clarifying the children's thinking about touching behaviors.

It is very helpful to play *Let's Talk About Touching* with the child with sexual behavior problems and their parents. It is also very useful to play this with all of the family members. This is a way for all family members to understand the issues around touching problems and to provide an additional prevention tool for sibling incest. It can also be helpful in individual, group, family, and multifamily group therapy.

EXERCISE ONE:
DIFFERENTIATING SEXUAL PLAY
FROM SEXUAL ABUSE

Materials:

Newsprint and stand
Wide Markers

1. Put up a large sheet of paper. Ask the children what sexual behaviors it is all right for children to engage in. Talk about children's natural and healthy curiosity. Normalize sexual exploration. Talk about sexual feelings that some children may have experienced.

2. Ask the children to make suggestions for behaviors that may be considered sexual play and those that might be considered abusive. Ask the children what is the difference between sexual play or sexual curiosity and sexually abusive behavior between children.

As the children go through the behaviors, help them to deduce that almost any behavior can be abusive. It is not necessarily the behavior itself (although adult sexual behavior is not all right for children to engage in) but the characteristics of the sexual interaction which make it abusive. For instance, if a child wants to hold hands with another child but the other child does not want to and the first child threatens to hurt the other child if he or she won't let him or her; this is harmful to the child. The behavior in and of itself is not a problem, but the threat coupled with sexuality is wrong. If a girl wants to see what a boy's penis looks like and she, together with another girl, pull down the boy's pants, this is not okay. Seeing a boy's penis is not wrong, but forcing someone to show theirs is wrong.

Appendix A has information that may be helpful as background for this exercise.

3. Put up another sheet of paper. Present either of the two examples above and make up others pertinent to the facility. Ask the children to make a list of what makes one situation all right and another abusive. The learning is much greater if the children try to find the answers themselves.

The following questions about characteristics of the sexual behavior, characteristics of the children engaged in the sexual behaviors, and characteristics of the process leading to the sexual behavior can be helpful in eliciting the factors that make a sexual behavior abusive, sexual play, or experimentation.

- Do both children understand and agree to what they are going to do before they start?
- Can both children decide about the sexual behavior they will do or does one child make all of the decisions?
- Do the children decide together to do the sexual behavior or does one child have the idea and badger the other child into doing it?
- What happens when one child wants to stop? Can either child decide when to stop?
- Does one child have to bribe the other child to do the behavior because the other child doesn't want to do it and has refused?
- What types of bribes are used? (Gifts, be on their team, extra food, be their best friend?)
- Does one child tell the other child they will hurt them if they don't do it?
- If one child has a hard time understanding things, does the other child take advantage of this? Is one child more likely to get picked on (vulnerable)? Is that why the child was chosen?
- Is one child a manipulator who gets others to do things they don't want to? Is one child being manipulated?

- If threats are used, does the child only do the behavior because he or she is afraid?
- Does one child have power or authority over the other and use it to make the child engage in the behavior? (Baby-sitter, older, bully?)
- Do the intentions of the children make a difference? Is it possible that one child may have very different intentions than the other child? Why do kids want to get other kids to do sexual things with them?
- What are the children's feelings about doing the sexual behaviors? Does this make a difference?
- Has one of the children been sexually victimized? Does this make a difference in how the child might feel?
- Does the age difference between the children make a difference?
- Is trying to force or tease a child into doing a sexual behavior the same as trying to get a child to steal a cookie or go out after dark without permission?
- Ask them to think about whether the relationship between the children has anything to do with trying to decide if something is sexual play or abusive.

    — Does it matter if the children are friends?
    — If they usually play together?
    — If one always bosses the other?
    — Does it matter if they generally like each other?

- If engaging in a sexual behavior is being used as an initiation into a group or a club does that make it all right or can it be abusive?
- Does one child "groom" another child? (See Chapter 7, Exercise Two)

EXERCISE TWO:
LET'S TALK ABOUT TOUCHING

Materials:

Game: *Let's Talk About Touching*

1. Begin the session by explaining the rules of the *Let's Talk About Touching* game. The adult explains that there are two kinds of cards: "Problem" cards and "Solution" cards. The object of the game is to find pairs, one "Problem" card and one "Solution" card with the same number, and to provide a thoughtful solution. When all of the pairs are matched, the person with the most pairs wins.

2. The game can be played like the classic game of concentration, described below, or it can be played like "Go Fish."

3. To Play: Place all or a portion* of the cards on the table with the "Problem" and "Solution" side showing. The players decide who will go first. Each player in turn selects a "Problem" card and a "Solution" card. If the cards do not have the same number, play proceeds clockwise. If the two cards have the same number, the player has a match. The player should then read the "Problem" card. After reading the card the player answers to the best of his/her ability. Other players can help if the player wants assistance. All players can ask questions or comment on another player's answer. After the answer is given, the "Solution" card can be read to the group. There may be more discussion at this time. The completed pair is placed in front of the player who found it.

The game is designed to allow the children to project themselves into many of the situations. The adult can listen for this to help define the relevant issues for each player.

---

*Depending on the age, impulse control, and frustration tolerance of the group, adults can decide how many pairs of cards to use. With younger children, seven to twelve pairs may be sufficient. The adult may wish to play with the other portion of the cards during another session. (There are 40 pairs of cards.)

Chapter 5

Personal Space

OBJECTIVES

- To make children conscious of their own and others' emotional, physical, and sexual boundaries.
- To make children aware of "space invasion."
- To teach children how to recognize and stop people if they violate their "space."
- To understand the concept of "privacy."

RATIONALE AND PURPOSE

Children who have been abused, neglected, and/or abandoned have generally lived in homes with people who themselves have significant difficulties. Among the issues which often arise in these homes is a lack of appreciation of other people's needs for personal space. People need their own emotional, physical, and sexual space and must respect others' space. One of the tasks of parents is to teach children about their own rights to personal space and physical privacy, as well as the rights of others.

Parents generally teach their children the rules regarding privacy. Yet, in some families, people do not have a right to physical privacy. Unfortunately, the rules may change in some homes, depending on who is in charge or whose privacy is being protected. Generally, adults have the right to privacy in their bedroom and in the bathroom. While children old enough to care for themselves should also have privacy, this is not always the case. Children are often confused about privacy because of the lack of clarity in their homes. Children who have been sexually abused in their bedrooms by an adult entering the room at night after they are asleep, or in the bathroom when they were bathing may have difficulty understanding the rules about privacy.

Privacy is one issue related to physical boundaries. Another is an individual's right to his/her personal space. Personal space is an invisible area around an individual that doesn't have a definite measurement but the person knows when it is being invaded. Personal space is less an issue between children than between children and adults. Children rough house and sit squeezed together in cars or when watching TV. Some out-of-home care facilities try to keep children physically separate at all times. This is unnatural for children and often takes a lot of supervision by staff. The utility of no physical contact between children should be carefully assessed. Trying to keep the children apart totally may increase the salience of the physical contact to an unnatural craving.

As children develop, the amount of personal space they require expands. Infants hug the adult's body, toddlers are carried, preschool children hold the parent's hand, elementary school children may walk side-by-side, and the teenager goes out with the family car! If family members do not have good emotional boundaries, this may be reflected in poor personal space boundaries. When there is a merging or fusing in the emotional area, there may be personal space invasion. Parents may invite the children into their bed, or bathe/shower with them long after the children require help and the children may feel uncomfortable with the nudity. The parents may persist in assisting children with their personal hygiene long after the children can take care of themselves.

In some families children do not learn about people's physical space requirements. Children will run right up to people and get in their face to talk to them, grab their arm, sit on their lap, ask for a hug from unknown people or people with whom they do not have a relationship, or go in someone's purse. The children are unaware that this can be perceived by another as a space violation. Likewise, the children do not know what personal space they should be able to insist on.

Emotional boundaries are violated when a person cannot have private thoughts and when others' feelings are projected onto them. When there are role reversals in the home, the children's emotional boundaries are disregarded. In some families with poor boundaries, children are placed in the role of protector of a parent, are told the details of the parents' problems, and become the friend or confidante of the parent. Sexual boundary violations include children being told the sexual intimacies of the parent, being put in the role of the surrogate boyfriend/girlfriend, observing intimate sexual behaviors by the parents, and being encouraged to act in sexually seductive ways.

Privacy is very difficult in out-of-home care. In many respects the children live as if they were in a goldfish bowl. They are often unable to have privacy for thoughts, possessions, toileting, or bathing. Adults can go in their rooms to search and caregivers and clinicians often try to get into their thoughts to figure out what they are thinking and feeling. Bathroom time also may not be private. Some out-of-home care facilities do not have doors on toilet stalls. Bedrooms are generally shared, and if not, doors are often left open. Children have little or no control over their lives. This is a very unnatural state but may well mimic their own home.

The need for close supervision is clear in out-of-home care. It will be useful though, to determine if there are some areas where there could be more privacy. Perhaps children could earn the right to have totally private possessions or totally solitary bathing and toileting privileges. Living with absolutely no privacy and environmental control may make it difficult for children to learn good boundaries.

GENERAL INSTRUCTIONS

There are two sessions. Read both before starting in order to become acquainted with the material.

It is important that the staff who work with the children understand this exercise so that the language and the ideas translate to the milieu. This exercise is to encourage the children to be *aware* and make *choices* about *space* and *privacy* for themselves and for others.

EXERCISE ONE:
PERSONAL COMFORT ZONES

Materials:

Tape Measure
Newsprint and stand
Wide Markers

1. Ask for a volunteer. The volunteer will stand in front of the group. A second volunteer is requested. This volunteer is told to go to the first child in order to ask a question. For example, the child might ask what is the other child's favorite breakfast, lunch, and dinner or the child's favorite songs, or favorite movies, etc. The idea is to have the two children talk for several minutes. After they start to talk, and seem to have come to their comfortable resting place for talking, they are told to remain standing where they are. One of the leaders goes with a tape measure and measures the distance between the two children. Measure the distance between the closest part of their bodies. Write this down. Note if either child touches the other during the questioning. The children will wonder what is going on. They can guess, but don't tell them until Step 5.

2. Ask for another set of volunteers. This is best done in an area with sofas or pillows on which the children can sit, or simply sit directly on the floor. Redo the exercise as in Step 1, except with one child sitting down and the other child going to the already seated child and sitting down to ask questions. Measure the distance between the closest part of their bodies. Note if either touches the other. Document this.

3. Have two adults do the same exercise. Measure the distance between the closest part of their bodies. Note if either touches the other. Document this.

4. This time have a leader stand and have one of the children walk up to ask a question. Follow the measuring procedure.

5. In the next sequence have a leader sit down and have a child come and sit to ask the leader a question. Measure. Document.

6. Now that all of the data is gathered, draw each of the participants on the newsprint, as stick figures (with names), the approximate distance they were from one another during the exercises. Label each of the figures by the child or adult's name. Let everyone examine the results.

- Ask participants if they were comfortable with the distance between them during the exercise. If they were not comfortable, what did they do? Does it ever happen in real life that you are uncomfortable but don't know what to do? (Some victims are unclear about what they deserve. Some victims do not feel they have the right to ask for what they want.)
- Do children stand closer to other children than they stand to adults? Why is this? Why not?
- Do children stand closer to each other when talking or do adults?
- Did people sit closer together or stand closer together to talk?
- How did the people in the exercise decide how close or far away they would stand or sit?

- Do people who know one another stand closer together or farther apart? Does knowing the other person make any difference?
- Do different people have different requirements for comfortable distance? Are some people more comfortable with people farther away from them? Closer to them?

7. Explain that the distance people like others to stand or sit from them is their personal space comfort zone. Different people have different personal space requirements. It may be interesting to the children that different cultural groups have different space requirements.

8. Children should understand that when people get too close it can feel uncomfortable. Explain the importance of knowing one's own personal space comfort zone requirements. Examples can be sought of people invading their personal space comfort zone. If the exercise on the continuum of physical touch has been done in Chapter 3, the children may be able to see the connection between some of the uncomfortable or abusive touches they have received and relate it to violations of their personal space comfort zone.

9. Children may want to "measure" the distance between people in the facility. They can be encouraged to pay attention to this in the milieu. Some children enjoy pointing out "space invaders!"

EXERCISE TWO:
SPACE INVADERS

Materials:

Newsprint and stand
Wide Markers

1. This exercise concerns physical privacy. The children have seen signs which say "private." Ask them where they have seen

these signs. "Private" signs are often on people's offices, on doors on the projection room in movie theaters, on bathrooms, on diaries, where special equipment is kept in gymnasiums, different places in factories where people might get hurt, etc.

2. Ask the children if there are signs in their homes which say "private." Generally, there are no signs but there is an unspoken consensus in the house about what and where is private. Different homes will have different rules. Some homes will have rules for children but not parents. Often children know their parents'/caretakers' bedroom is "private," if the door is closed, but there may be no reciprocity. Ask the children for places and times where people have privacy in their home. Examples could be: privacy in the bathroom to use the toilet, privacy of one's personal items such as letters, thoughts, and feelings. Stress that all people may have thoughts and feelings which they do not want to share with others. Private thoughts are important and the person can decide when they feel comfortable sharing the thoughts and feelings. Private things can be our bedroom, bathroom, desk drawers, or toys; or personal items such as clothes, soap, toothbrush; or any part of our body, including skin, hair, the clothes we have on, private parts, etc.

3. Some children's personal space comfort zone may be too broad. Talk about knowing when someone is violating the child's personal space.

- What are some of the ways we know when someone invades our personal space?
- Have you ever felt like someone gets too close to you to talk? Have you ever felt yourself backing away from someone because they seemed to close?
- Are there feelings you get when someone invades your personal space?
- Are there any people in the facility who invade your personal space?

- Are the rules about privacy different in the facility and your home? Which rules do you like better?
- What types of things do you like to keep private?
- Do you feel you have privacy in the facility? Did you have any privacy at home?
- What do you do when someone invades your personal space?

4. Relate this issue of a personal space comfort zone to their responsibility to realize the personal space requirements of others.

- What signals have you gotten that you have invaded others' personal space comfort zones?
- Has anyone ever told on you for "space invasion?"
- When someone got upset with you for a "space invasion," were you aware you were invading their space or did you need them to tell you? Some kids have not learned the unwritten rules about privacy and space invasion. It is never too late to learn.
- Sometimes do you just break the "space invasion" rules, even though you know you are doing it? If so, why? If not, how do you prevent yourself from doing this?

5. For homework children can make a list of all the ways others invade their privacy. Another list should be made of ways they invade the privacy of others. A point for each example can get them more points on the behavior chart for generalization.

Chapter 6

Sexual Knowledge

OBJECTIVES

- To provide children with basic information regarding their bodies.
- To name the body parts.
- To normalize the sexual parts of the body.
- To encourage healthy sexual knowledge in children.
- To name the body parts that are private. To assure that the children are aware of their right to make their own decisions about who does what to their body. To assure the children are aware of their responsibility to respect other people's private parts, both children and adults.
- To discuss the function of the sexual body parts.
- To model openness when talking about the body, sexuality, and sexual behaviors.
- To reinforce the children's rights and decision making about their own body.

RATIONALE AND PURPOSE

Children generally lack information about all body parts and in particular the sexual body parts. Correct information can assist the children to develop healthy attitudes and understanding about sex and sexuality.

The issue of choices about how private parts are used will be a major topic. We must not assume that children know that they can refuse to have people touch their bodies, including their private parts.

This exercise is to assure that the children have a good knowledge of their bodies and the rules that they make about them. It will be particularly important to encourage questions by the children. This will be a good way to understand areas of concern for them. Incorrect information can lead to sexual confusion. Sexual confusion may lead to sexual acting out.

As this can be a very difficult area for children who have been sexually abused and for children with any kind of sexual behavior problem, attend closely to their knowledge and affect. Frequently, sexually abused children have a great deal of misinformation about sex. This can often be a source of distress to them. For instance, girls may worry about whether they are pregnant. Body image may come up in the discussion. Some children believe others can tell they have been sexually abused if they see them nude. Boys often worry about homosexuality. Frequently street terms for body parts are misunderstood by children. This can be straightened out. Anything that comes up in the discussion should be talked about openly and clearly.

These four exercises are brief and focused on some of the information children need. They are included for out-of-home facilities that do not have full sexuality curricula for the children. A more detailed curriculum for children on sex and sexuality is available. Exercises Three and Four can be reversed.

EXERCISE ONE:
BODY PARTS

Materials:

Newsprint and stand
Wide Markers

1. Draw an outline of two bodies with no identifying physical markers. The bodies can be of the gingerbread man style. Ask the

children to give the name of any body part. A group leader writes the body parts on the newsprint. The group is encouraged to find as many body parts as possible, e.g., knuckles, cuticles, hangnails, earlobes, eyelashes, etc. If the children use slang or derogatory words for body parts write them down and ask for other terms with the same meaning. Put the words side-by-side. Make no particular comment at the time.

2. After the children have done as many body parts as they can think of, ask them which parts on the list are considered the parts involved in sexual behaviors. Put an asterisk next to the parts which are considered sexual. If the children did not get down all of the sexual body parts, fill in the rest at this time.

Some children will include parts of the body as sexual that the adults may not have thought of as sexual, such as skin, mouth, fingers, tongue, etc. List all parts of the body the children say are sexual.

3. Ask the children to describe what is meant by sexual. A discussion of why they say these are sexual parts of the body will frequently lead the leaders to greater insights concerning how the children view sexuality. The leader should take every opportunity to ascribe healthy, happy, and important functions to people's sexuality.

4. When it seems applicable to the group, ask what words their friends use for the private parts, or what words are used in songs, on videos, and on the street. If the children have given slang words during the exercise, write them down at this time. When a slang term is used make sure that the proper term is put beside it. In one group a boy kept using "pussy." When asked for the proper term he said "Puddy Kat!" We cannot always be sure that street talk is understood.

5. Examine the list of alternate words. See what can be drawn from this list. Are the words appealing, kind, angry, derogatory, or symbols of disgust? Discuss why this may be. Are people

comfortable with their sexuality? Encourage the children to see sexuality as an important and positive part of each person.

6. Encourage the use of proper terminology or nonderogatory slang for the sexual body parts.

EXERCISE TWO:
THE FUNCTION OF THE SEXUAL PARTS

Materials:

Newsprint and stand
Wide Markers

1. Draw an outline of two bodies with no identifying physical markers. Use the list of private parts developed in the previous session. Write the name of the private part on the paper near the body area. Give the proper names for the private parts. Include: penis, testicles, scrotum, vulva, vagina, uterus, breasts, nipples, mouth, buttocks, and anus.

2. Ask the children to describe the function of each of the sexual body parts. Remark that the penis is used in going to the bathroom and delivering sperm to the vagina. Explain the general outline of how the sexual body parts are used in sexual acts to make babies. Describe the function of the breasts to feed infants. Ask (and answer) all questions the children have. Remember that children may be very reluctant to ask questions in this area. Leaders may wish to pose some questions to get the children started. "Have you ever wondered what parts of the body are involved in making babies?" The leaders may want to read the books listed in Exercise Four for background information before this exercise.

3. Describe the sexual body parts as private. Impress on the children their right to make all decisions regarding their own private parts. Help the children see their responsibility in making

decisions about what they do with their private parts and the need to respect the right of others to make decisions about their body parts.

4. The children can be asked about any problems they think may happen more in out-of-home care than at home, or more at home than in out-of-home care regarding the private parts of the body. This can be a general question to see if it elicits response. If there are known problems in the facility regarding the touching of private parts this may be a good opportunity for an open discussion.

EXERCISE THREE: WHERE DO I COME FROM?

Materials:

Video: *Where Do I Come From?* (Available in most video stores.)

1. Watch the video.
2. Ask for questions and comments.
3. Foster discussion among the children. Elicit as much discussion as possible, as the confusion or misinterpretations will become evident in this way. It will be important to help the children develop a clear understanding of the sexual and reproductive system as many concerns focus on this area.

- Was there anything that surprised you?
- When you first heard sexual information was it correct?
- Did your parents tell you the facts of life?
- Will you tell your children?

EXERCISE FOUR:
AS YOU GROW UP

Materials:

Books published by Channing L. Bete titled *As Boys Grow Up*, *As Girls Grow Up,* and *As You Grow Up* have very good material for this exercise. It may be best to photocopy the pages relating to the body parts and distribute the entire booklet for the following exercise on puberty. If the booklet is given out with this exercise it may be lost, destroyed, stolen, or dog-eared by the next session on puberty. See Ordering Supplementary Materials pp. 19-20.

Use *As Boys Grow Up, As Girls Grow Up*, or *As You Grow Up.* Go through a little at a time. Encourage the children to read out loud, if they can. The more questions the leader can bring forth from the child, the more the leader will understand any confusion the child has and what needs to be explained.

Chapter 7

Prevention of Sexual Misuse
or Abuse

OBJECTIVES

- To give children practice in identifying situations that may lead to abuse.
- To teach children some rules to help them from being hurt by others.
- To help children understand the "grooming" done by offenders.
- To assist children to know the ways they can be manipulated into sexual behavior.
- To assist children to understand how offenders keep children from telling.
- To encourage children to use trusted adults as resources to ask for advice when they are not sure about something.
- To sensitize children regarding the seriousness of making abuse allegations.
- To assure children know who to go to for help if they think something or someone is unsafe.
- To have children help other children by making a prevention pamphlet.

RATIONALE AND PURPOSE

Child sexual abuse and misuse occurs all too frequently in our society. Offenders look for vulnerable children, i.e., children who appear emotionally needy. Vulnerability can come from a lack of emotional comfort, love, and connectedness to family members. Sex offenders generally develop a relationship with children prior to molesting them. Vulnerable children are susceptible to someone who says he or she cares and offers the children emotional closeness. The children often get entrapped by the positive closeness before the offender engages in any sexual behavior. The emotional relationship, fun, bribes, coercive statements, and threats make it extremely hard for the child to tell after the sexual behavior begins. Many children say that they like the perpetrator, they just wish there was no sexual behavior involved.

Many adolescent perpetrators get children involved in sex behaviors in the same way as adult sex offenders. Alert the children that adolescents as well as children may attempt to molest them. They must be alert to any sign of danger, learn their own body signals which will alert them that they are nervous or uncomfortable, and learn to engage in an internal dialog about their situation. Children must be aware that some people who sexually molest children may be members of their immediate or extended family. While this is hard to discuss with children, it is important that it be raised.

Some offenders take (grab) children and hurt them without developing a relationship with them. While this is the minority of offenders, children must be aware of this also.

Prevention exercises provided in the family are very beneficial. Exercises can help sensitize parents to preventing abuse to their children. Asking the parents to focus on how offenders find their victims and manipulate them into silence will assist their understanding of the process and help them to protect their children. This may be new information to the parents. The parents and children could do these plays together in multifamily groups and have a great time. It is important to do some prevention work with parents before children return home.

EXERCISE ONE:
LEARNING ABOUT PREVENTION THROUGH PLAYS

1. Children are told that they will do plays related to different topics. *Some* of the topics will involve helping them be aware of situations when someone may be trying to engage them in an unsafe situation. Tell the children that some of the plays will not be about abuse or potential abuse so that the children will have to try to figure out if it is a dangerous situation or not. Children will take turns being the major player.

2. A child is chosen. The leader can give this child a choice between two or three of the vignettes. The child decides how to do the play. The child can select group members to be in the play, tell them their roles and the basic thrust of the play, but not exactly what to say or do. The selected group members act in their role according to what is going on in the play. Encourage the children to stay in role and say what they really would say in such a situation. Try to make it as real life as possible. The vignettes are to be used as the beginning of the action in the play. Have the participants act out what is written and then continue the scenario to a logical conclusion. As the children continue the play, the leader will better understand how they conceptualize the issues. Remind the children that the vignettes may or may not lead to abuse depending on what the actors do. Encourage the children to make some vignettes lead to abuse and others not so they can try to learn what are the danger signs.

If the play is too stereotypical, the leader can insert another character or a twist to the scenario to make the children deal with an unforeseen situation. For instance, in Scenario Five, if the child says "no" to the first attempt at getting him/her into the trailer, whisper to the person playing the adult to think of something that would attract the child. For example, the adult might suggest $10.00 as an added incentive. Get the children to think of what might entice them.

In the first role-play below, the child who is the major player can tell two other children that they are playing in a park and nothing else. The child who is the major player assumes the role of the stranger, draws a picture of a dog, gets a prop for a leash and proceeds to try to get the children to go look for the dog with him.

3. Below are some suggestions for scenarios. The children may want to make up their own. Make up any which seem pertinent to the children's circumstances.

4. If you plan to do Exercise Four in this module, tell the children that they should be thinking about what kind of rules or suggestions they can make to other children to help them be safe. This information will come from what they learn doing the vignettes. If they want, they can write down the rules and suggestions as they go along.

5. After the vignette has come to a conclusion, ask the children:

- What things led them to believe something bad might happen?
- What things made them think the situation was safe?
- What things did you learn about how people try to trap children into situations in which abuse might occur?

Scenarios:

Juan is playing in the park. A stranger comes up carrying a leash and shows him a picture of his dog. The stranger says his name is George and asks if Juan has seen the dog. George says the dog just got away and he thinks he is just over on the other side of the hill. Since George can't move very fast, he asks if Juan and his friends will help him look for the dog. George is very friendly and nice.

Jerome's teacher takes him to the arcade one afternoon. Jerome is not sure why he got to do that special activity. The next day in class Jerome does not do his work and the teacher gets mad at him. Jerome thought maybe he was special and could get away with anything he wanted. The teacher asks Jerome if he wants to go to Burger King next week. Jerome wonders _____.

Brian is playing on the jungle gym. A woman who Brian doesn't know comes up and says that Brian's mother has asked her to bring him home. The woman says that Brian's mother will have to be a little late so they will go to McDonald's on the way to Brian's home. Brian wants to go to McDonald's because they have a great playground.

Your uncle, age 16, is really nice and likes to play with young kids. You like to play with him. You are outside playing baseball. Some of your uncles' friends come by. One of his friends, Trevor, asks you to go to his house with him to pick up some candy. You don't know Trevor and suggest that two of your friends come along. Trevor says "No, lets just you and I go, I have some candy at home; you can eat some on the way back." You decide to go. On the way back _____.

You are in a shopping mall with your friends. A man comes up and says he is looking for models for a commercial. He says you look just like the kind of kid he needs. He has a trailer outside where he is doing screen tests. You _____.

Derrick's therapist keeps asking him about sexual things that happened to him when he was little. He says he doesn't want to talk about it. It makes him very uncomfortable. His therapist keeps asking. Derrick _____.

Sam is in the video arcade playing his favorite video game. A teenager named Jose, who is a friend of Sam's brother, keeps putting quarters in the machine so Sam can keep playing. Sam wonders why Jose is doing this, but doesn't ask. They finally run out of money. Jose asks Sam if he wants to go play video games at his home. Sam _____.

John is in an ice cream store. The manager offers him a free ice cream sundae if he will clean all the tables. John really wants the ice cream. John _____.

Your stepmother keeps coming in the bathroom when you are using the toilet. It embarrasses you because you don't like it when people see you going to the bathroom. You are not sure why she comes in. You are also not sure what will happen if you ask her to stop. Your dad may be mad at you. You think about it a lot and decide to _____.

One of the staff you really like said that maybe you could be his foster child and live with him. You really like that idea. The staff person says you have to keep it quiet because it is against the rules. You wonder how he could do it if it is against the rules. You are not sure that you should keep this secret. You decide to _____.

A boy in your foster home wants you to help him steal cake from the kitchen. You agree. After you do that, he says he wants to touch your privates. You say "no." He says he will tell that you stole the cake from the kitchen. You _____. The boy then _____.

The group home supervisor, Jim, is really nice to Tom. Tom likes him. Sometimes Jim takes Tom home with him when he has to pick up something. Tom likes to go to Jim's house because Jim lets him play Nintendo as long as he wants. He doesn't have to share with anyone. Jim tells Tom that he will get in trouble if Tom says that he has been to Jim's house. Tom talks to one of his cottagemates about this. The cottagemate says_____.

A staff person takes you to the store. You know that the rule is that there is supposed to be two children when you go off campus with a staff. The staff person then takes you to a video arcade and gives you lots of quarters. You can't figure out what is going on. You try to figure out what is going on by asking questions of the staff person.

John has been doing very well in the group home. He has gotten all of his points for a long time and is on the highest level of the behavioral system. His therapist, Debby, says they can go to the movies. John thought that they could only go to the mall but not to the movies. John asks, "What movie?" Then _____.

A caregiver lets Trevor, age 8, stay up late. After all the children are asleep, the caregiver comes in Trevor's room and reads him a book. The caregiver tells Trevor he must keep this special time a secret. The following night the caregiver comes into Trevor's room and asks if he wants another book read to him. Trevor really likes the books. He _____. The caregiver then _____.

A policewoman comes to the residential center. She is in uniform and has a gun. She talks to your social worker. The police officer wants to ask you some questions. The policewoman wants to take you in a room by herself. You feel uncomfortable. You decide to _____.

EXERCISE TWO:
GROOMING AND THREATS

Materials:

Newsprint and stand
Markers

This session is designed to help children understand the "grooming" process of sex offenders as well as the threats and bribes which are used to keep children quiet.

1. "Grooming" is when the offender tries to make friends with the person with whom he or she wants to engage in sexual behaviors. The offender slowly makes friends with the child and frequently gives them things. Only gradually does the offender begin engaging the child in any sexual behaviors. When the sex

starts the child generally wants to keep getting the good things but have the sexual part go away. The trap has been set and it makes it very hard for the children to tell the person or to tell anyone else. As the sex offender engages the child in the sexual behaviors he or she may start the threats.

2. Ask the children to think of how children or adults have gotten them to do things they didn't really want to do. Make a list of these.

3. Ask the children all of the ways they know of that sex offenders get children to engage in the sexual behavior. See if there are similarities between the lists. Tell the children, "People of all ages molest children. Grown-ups, teenagers, and children sexually touch children in ways that are not okay. Look at the list you made. How many things on the list you already made are things people do to fool children into the sexual behaviors? We will make a list later of the things which offenders do to keep children from telling. Right now just think about the ways people fool children into doing sexual stuff."

Some of the ways sex offenders engage children in out-of-home care are the same as extrafamilial and intrafamilial sex offenders. Children should be wary of anyone in an out-of-home facility—child, teenager, or adult who:

- goes in their room with them and closes the door in order to have "private" talks.
- wants them to keep secrets about what they do together.
- gives them special gifts other children don't get.
- gives them special privileges other children don't get.
- wants to play games related to private parts or engage in sexual talk.
- gives them pictures of naked people or wants to take their picture without clothes on.
- insists that their relationship has to be "just between us."
- says they can live with them in the future.
- takes them to their house.

4. The second aspect for the children to understand is the threats or other coercive aspects of the abuse. Discuss threats that adults, teenagers, and children use to keep someone from telling about abuse. Ask the children to list all of the ways people (adults and kids) try to get other people (adults and kids) not to tell about something they did. This can be about stealing a cookie, hitting someone, taking drugs, etc.

5. After this list is completed, ask the children which of the ways on the list are methods used by sex offenders to keep children from telling. These can be checked off.

6. Then, ask the children to make another list of additional ways sex offenders get children not to tell.

Examples of threats are:

- If you tell, I'll say it was your fault.
- If you tell, I'll say you wanted to do it.
- You will spoil our fun if you tell.
- We won't be able to have any more fun if you tell.
- They will take me away and you won't get any more special favors.
- You are the one who will get in trouble, not me.
- I'll lose my job, if you tell.
- It will be your fault if I go to jail.
- You are the one who started this, you better be quiet or I'll tell on you.

Children who have been abused in their families may have heard "You'll destroy the family, if you tell on me," "Your mother won't believe you," or "You will hurt your mother, if she finds out."

7. During this exercise the reporting of suspected emotional, sexual, or physical abuse in out-of-home care should be discussed thoroughly. Children often think that they have to accept things that happen to them because they are little and powerless. Children should be encouraged to know that they can trust their

feelings and report when they think someone is doing something wrong to them. If they think a caregiver, another child in the residence, or anyone else is too physically harsh with them, or touches them in a way that makes them feel uncomfortable, they should tell someone who can help them.

8. Each child should know exactly what to do and to whom to speak. It is very important that children report a suspicion of emotional, sexual, or physical abuse. There are many times when children are not sure if they are being abused, they should be encouraged to speak up about this. The adults will help them to get a better understanding of the situation.

Children can help one another. If a child suspects that another child is being abused they should tell a trusted adult. Staff should understand that they are mandated reporters. If they know that any kind of abuse is occurring, they can be fined or sent to jail (depends on the law) for not reporting. It should be made clear that the reporting law requires reporting when there is a "suspicion" of abuse. The person telling does not need to know for sure, only be concerned or suspicious it is occurring.

EXERCISE THREE:
BEING ALERT

Materials:

Worksheets: *Ways We Show We Are Uncomfortable* (completed and blank)
Worksheets: *What Behaviors Are Suspicious?* (completed and blank)
Worksheets: *Questions to Ask Myself When I Am Uncomfortable* (completed and blank)

1. There are three exercises available. All worksheets are in Appendix C. The adults can decide which of the exercises they

want to do. This will depend on the needs of the children and their sophistication with prevention. The exercises are meant to stimulate the children to think. Many programs teach the children material that they are to memorize. These exercises are to encourage the children to think out the problem.

2. Using the worksheets: *What Behaviors Are Suspicious?* Ask the children to think about behaviors that someone who is trying to force, bribe, coerce, or tease a child into sexual behaviors might do. Remind the children that the person could be a child, teenager, or adult.

Read the filled in worksheet before starting the exercise. Give the children some examples to start them off. Then let them come up with examples about themselves, their parents/caretakers, and other people of all ages. They can think of examples from their favorite television characters.

3. Using the worksheets: *Ways We Show We Are Uncomfortable.* Ask the children all of the ways they can tell when they are uncomfortable. These are behavioral characteristics of the children. If the group has been together for a while, it will be fun for the children to try to remember times when they have seen the other children uncomfortable and try to recall what they did.

Tell the children that the point of this exercise is for them to be able to read their own body signals. When we can read our body signals we can be alerted to danger that we may have picked up unconsciously and need to bring into our conscious awareness. Also indicate that other people may have similar body signals when they are uncomfortable or nervous. If the children are with someone who is acting uncomfortable or anxious, it may alert them to be aware of what is going on. They may decide that they should leave or change the circumstances.

4. Using the worksheets: *Questions to Ask Myself When I Am Uncomfortable.* Ask the children all of the things they can ask themselves to determine if they are uncomfortable with what is happening or if they are in a dangerous situation. The answers to

this exercise form a part of the internal dialog in which the children can engage to make a decision about the safest course of action. Remind the children that the person creating the uncomfortable or dangerous situation could be a child, teenager, or adult.

5. The final part of the exercise is to ask the children what they will do if they feel uncomfortable. Try to get answers other than "leave the situation," as that may not always be possible. Find realistic answers.

EXERCISE FOUR:
FIGURING OUT THE RULES

Materials:

Poster paper
Wide pens
List of Rules to Keep You Safe

1. Tell the children that the purpose of the exercise is to review all they have learned about safety and develop a set of rules which will help other children to be safe. Encourage the children to think of what people say to get children to do things that may not be safe. Encourage the children to think of what types of situations they need to protect themselves in. The children can think about what gave them the idea during the plays of what was safe or unsafe. Use the poster paper to make a list of these things.

2. Many situations will not be straightforward. Some children may worry about who they can trust or how to make friends if everyone is suspect. Discuss these thoughts as you try to come up with some guidelines for children about being safe. Talk about how trust is built with people by watching what they do and by checking if they tell the truth, keep their word, and think about others not just themselves.

3. As the children struggle with rules which keep children safe, encourage discussion between them. Following are some rules the children should remember:

- Never go alone with someone you don't know, unless your parents or an adult you trust and have known for a long time says it is okay.
- Be alert to suspicious behaviors.
- If you feel uncomfortable with what someone is doing, pay attention to your feelings and change the situation.
- If someone wants you to be sexual with him/her, tell the person "no" and then tell someone you trust.
- If someone wants you to keep a secret that you know is not right, be suspicious.
- If someone offers you something really nice (food, money, presents, special privileges) for no good reason, be suspicious.
- When you are suspicious, ask someone you trust what they think about what happened. Get help if you need it.
- When you ask for help from someone you trust and that person does not really help, ask another adult you trust until you get the help you need.

4. List the specific people each child would choose to tell if he/she felt unsafe or suspicious and wanted help.

5. Ask children about any experiences they may have had with telling someone about something which happened to them. Sometimes children's reality has been shattered when they told about abuse and nothing happened. Encourage children to listen carefully to each other and learn from what they each say. As sex offenders often tell children no one will believe them, this information is important. If there are children who were not believed when they told, try to figure out the reasons. Ask what the child did to get the person to believe. If the person never

believed them, show empathy and then try to problem solve how to get help.

6. The material from this exercise should be shared with the child's parents before he or she returns home. The child and family will then share the same guidelines for preventing abuse. When children live at home it is good for everyone in the family to agree on a "password." If someone wanted to take the child somewhere that he did not know about, he would only go with a person who knew the "password."

EXERCISE FIVE: HELPING OTHER CHILDREN

Materials:

Video camera
Paper
Markers
Photocopy machine
Writing pens

1. Suggest to the children that they put together a prevention pamphlet, a TV-type commercial, develop a slogan, make up a play, or in some way devise a method to help other children. Let the group decide what type of prevention they will develop and what they want to prevent.

2. Ask the children to think of what they have learned and what they wish they had known when they were younger that may have prevented them from being harmed. Encourage them to want to help other children. There may be some discussion about the feelings they have about their lives and ways to prevent other children from being hurt.

References

Bloom, R. B. (1992). "When staff members sexually abuse children in residential care." *Child Welfare, 71*(2): 131-145.

Budin, L. and Johnson, C. F. (1989). "Sex abuse prevention programs: Offenders' attitudes about their efficacy." *Child Abuse & Neglect, 13*: 77-87.

Elliot, M., Browne, K., and Kilcoyne, J. (1995). "Child abuse prevention: What offenders tell us." *Child Abuse & Neglect, 19*: 579-594.

Finkelhor, D., Asdigian, N., and Dziuba-Leatherman. (1995). "The effectiveness of victimization prevention instruction: An evaluation of children's responses to actual threats and assaults." *Child Abuse & Neglect, 19*: 141-153.

Finkelhor, D. and Dziuba-Leatherman (1995). "Victimization prevention programs: A national survey of children's exposure and reactions." *Child Abuse & Neglect, 19*: 129-139.

Gil, E. (1982). Institutional abuse of children in out-of-home care. *Institutional Abuse of Children and Youth.* Binghamton, NY: The Haworth Press. 7-13.

Hargrave, M. C. (1991). "Sexual Incidents in residential treatment." *Child and Youth Care Forum, 20*(6): 413-419.

Navarre, E. L. (1983). Sexually abused children prevention, protection and care: A handbook for residential care facilities. Prepared for National Center on Child Abuse and Neglect, Washington, DC.

Wurtele, S. K., Gillispie, E. I., Currier, L., and Franklin, C. F. (1992). "A comparison of teachers vs. parents as instructors of a personal safety program for preschoolers." *Child Abuse & Neglect, 16*: 127-137.

Wurtele, S. K. and Miller-Perrin, C. L. (1992). *Preventing sexual abuse: Sharing the responsibility.* Lincoln, NE: University of Nebraska Press.

Appendix A

Children's Sexual Behaviors

When presented with a child who is engaging in sexual behaviors, parents, teachers, medical professionals, mental health professionals, school and public health nurses, and others who come in contact with children, sometimes find it difficult to decide when a child's sexual behavior is to be expected and when it may be an indication of some distress or disturbance. This paper provides a definition of natural and healthy childhood sexual behaviors. In addition, characteristics of children's sexual behaviors are described which may alert adults that an assessment of the child may be indicated. The level of concern regarding the child increases in direct proportion to the number and type of the characteristics which fit the child's sexual behaviors.

It is important to bear in mind that children's sexual behaviors, as well as their level of comfort with sexuality will be affected by the amount of exposure to adult sexuality, nudity, explicit television, videos, and pictures; the amount of space in which the family lives; and the child's level of sexual interest. Parental, cultural, societal, and religious attitudes and values will also influence children's sexual behavior and attitudes.

NATURAL AND HEALTHY
SEXUAL BEHAVIORS

Natural and healthy sexual exploration during childhood is an *information gathering process* wherein children *explore* each other's bodies, by looking and touching (e.g., playing doctor), as well as explore *gender roles and behaviors* (e.g., playing house). Children involved in natural and expected sex play are of *similar age, size, and developmental status* and participate on a *voluntary* basis. While siblings engage in *mutual* sexual exploration, most sex play is between children who have an ongoing mutually enjoyable play and/or school *friendship*. The sexual behaviors are *limited in type and frequency* and occur in *several periods* of the child's life. The child's interest in sex and sexuality is *balanced* by curiosity about other aspects of his or her life. Natural and expected sexual exploration may result in *embarrassment* but does not usually leave children with deep feelings of anger, shame, fear, or anxiety. If the children are discovered in sexual exploration and instructed to stop, the behavior generally *diminishes, at least in the view of adults*. The feelings of the children regarding the sexual behavior is generally *light-hearted and spontaneous*. Generally, children experience pleasurable sensations from genital touching, some children experience sexual arousal, while some children experience orgasm. Sexual arousal and orgasm are more frequently found in older children entering puberty.

TWENTY CHARACTERISTICS OF PROBLEMATIC SEXUAL BEHAVIOR

The following characteristics can be used to assess whether a child is engaging in sexual behaviors that may require a professional evaluation. If a child's sexual behavior can be described by several of the following characteristics and the child's caretakers cannot find a reasonable explanation for this, the child should be evaluated by a qualified professional who is knowledgeable about child sexuality or child abuse and, perhaps, have a medical examination. A child-sensitive interview regarding possible confusion about sexuality, misuse, neglect, or abuse is indicated, bearing in mind that there are many reasons for problematic sexual behaviors. (See above.)

1. *The children engaged in the sexual behaviors do not have an ongoing mutual play relationship.* Sexual play between children is an extension of regular play behavior. Just as children prefer to play with children with whom they get along, this is the same with sexual play. As most children are very aware of taboos on sexual play in the open, they pick friends who will keep the secret.

2. *Sexual behaviors that are engaged in by children of different ages or developmental levels.* Unless there are no similar age children in the neighborhood, most children select playmates of the same age. Yet, developmentally delayed children may choose to play with younger children because their developmental level is more similar. Children with poor social skills may also play with younger children. It will be important to assess availability of peer-age friends, developmental level, and the previous relationship between the children to determine if sexual behaviors between children of different ages are problematic. In general, the wider the age difference, the greater the concern.

3. *Sexual behaviors that are out of balance with other aspects of the child's life and interests.* Children are interested in every aspect of their environment from the sun rising to how babies are made. While children may explore some aspects of their world more extensively at certain periods of their young lives, their interests are generally broad and intermittent. Children's sexual behavior follows the same pattern. At one period they may be very interested in learning about sexuality and another time about how the dishwasher works or what will make Mommy mad. Many fluctuations occur in a day, a week,

and a month. When a child is preoccupied with sexuality, this raises concern. If a child would prefer to masturbate rather than engage in regular childhood activities, this raises concern.

4. *Children who seem to have too much knowledge about sexuality and behave in ways more consistent with adult sexual expression.* As children develop, they acquire knowledge about sex and sexuality from television, movies, videos, magazines, their parents, relatives, school, and other children. Knowledge gathered in these time-honored ways is generally assimilated, without disruption, into the child's developing understanding of sex and sexuality; this translates into additional natural and healthy sexual interest. When children have been overexposed to explicit adult sexuality, or have been sexually misused, they may engage in or talk about sexual behaviors that are beyond age-appropriate sexual knowledge and interest.

5. *Sexual behaviors that are significantly different than those of other same-age children.* The frequency and type of children's sexual behaviors depend, to a certain extent, on the environment (home, neighborhood, culture, religion) in which they have been raised, their parent's attitudes and actions related to sex and sexuality, and their peers' behaviors. If a child's sexual behavior stands out among his or her neighborhood peers, this raises concern. Teachers from schools that serve neighborhood populations are very good resources to consult to evaluate whether a child's sexual behaviors are similar to his or her peers.

6. *Sexual behaviors that continue in spite of consistent and clear requests to stop.* While adults may be inconsistent regarding other behaviors, and children may persist in engaging in them, children generally learn very quickly that

there is a strong taboo on openly sexual behavior. While most adults are consistent about telling children to stop, some are not. Inconsistent messages regarding sexual behavior may increase or not decrease, a child's sexual behaviors.

Children's sexual behaviors that continue in the view of adults, despite consistent requests to stop or even punishment, may be a conscious or unconscious method of indicating that they need help. When children "cry for help" they may persist in the behavior until adults pay heed, discover, and/or change the causes of the sexual behavior. Sometimes children who are being sexually abused signal the abuse by engaging in persistent sexual behaviors.

Some children have learned to "space out" in times of stress. While they are "spaced out" they may engage in sexual behavior which itself is a way to decrease their anxiety. If this is happening, the child may be unaware of what he or she is doing. Because the child's response to stress is to "space out" and engage in sexual behaviors, it may happen in spite of consistent requests to stop.

7. *Children who appear unable to stop themselves from engaging in sexual activities.* Some children appear to feel driven to engage in sexual behaviors even though they will be punished or admonished. Generally, this type of sexual behavior is in response to things that go on around them or feelings that reawaken memories that are traumatic, painful, overly stimulating, or of which they can't make sense. The child may respond directly by masturbating or engaging in other sexual behaviors alone, with children, or with adults. Hiding the sexual behaviors or finding friends to engage in the behaviors in private, may not be possible for these children. Anxiety-, guilt-, or fear-driven sexual behavior often does not respond to normal limit setting. The sexual behav-

ior is a way of coping with overwhelming feelings. This type of sexual behavior is often not within the full conscious control of the child.

Some children who engage in the more compulsive sexual behaviors may have an excess of sex hormones or other physiological differences that cause this behavior.

8. *Children's sexual behaviors that are eliciting complaints from other children and/or adversely affecting other children.* Generally, children complain when something is annoying or discomforting to them. When a young child complains about another child's sexual behaviors, it is an indication that the behavior is upsetting to the child and should be taken seriously. In natural and healthy sexual play both children agree directly or indirectly not to tell, and engage in it willingly. It is quite unlikely that either would tell on the other; therefore, if one child is telling, this is a cause for concern.

Alternatively, elementary school, opposite-gender children on school playgrounds run after one another discovering who has the most "cooties." When the children are equal in age, developmental status, and are having fun together, these complaints are a lively spirited interchange which need only be monitored to see that it remains fun and noncoercive.

9. *Children's sexual behaviors that are directed at adults who feel uncomfortable receiving them.* Children hug adults and give them kisses. These are generally spontaneous reflections of caring or because they have been told to kiss the adult (usually a relative) by a parent. When a child continues to touch an adult in a manner more like adult-adult sexual contact, offer themselves as sexual objects, or solicit sexual touch from adults, this raises concern.

10. *Children (four years and older) who do not understand their rights or the rights of others in relation to sexual contact.* Children who do not understand who has the right to touch their bodies or whose bodies they can touch, may not have grown up learning this. Some children may live with people who do not respect their emotional, physical, or sexual privacy. If a child is not given privacy, he or she will not give it to others. Sexual abuse often involves teaching children to touch others in a sexual way, as well as people touching their bodies whenever and however they want. Children may have been taught how to stimulate adults or other children, thus never being taught to respect others' bodies or that their own body should be respected.

11. *Sexual behaviors that progress in frequency, intensity, or intrusiveness over time.* While sexual behavior in children is natural and expected, the frequency is not generally high. It is sporadic and occurs outside the vision and knowledge of others. Since children's sexual behaviors generally become increasingly less visible to adults during early elementary school, if a child's sexual behaviors invade others' emotional and physical space, are increasing, and are known to adults, this raises concern.

12. *When fear, anxiety, deep shame, or intense guilt is associated with the sexual behaviors.* Children's feelings regarding sexuality is generally light-hearted, spontaneous, giggly, or silly. In some cases, if a child has been caught engaging in sexual behaviors, the adult's response may have generated embarrassed or guilty feelings in the child. Yet, these feelings are qualitatively different than the deep shame, intense guilt, fear, or anxiety of a child who has been fooled, coerced, bribed, or threatened into sexual behaviors or overexposed to adult sexuality.

13. *Children who engage in extensive, persistent mutually agreed upon adult-type sexual behaviors with other children.* Children generally engage in a variety of spontaneous and sporadic sexual behaviors with other children for purposes of exploration and the satisfaction of curiosity. Some children who feel alone in the world may turn to other children to decrease their loneliness. These children often do not see adults as sources of emotional warmth and caring. If the children have been prematurely sexualized and/or taught that sex equals caring, they may try to use sex as a way to cope with their loneliness.

14. *Children who manually stimulate or have oral or genital contact with animal/s.* Children in urban and suburban areas rarely have contact with the genitalia of animals. Children on farms might have some sexual contact with animals but it is limited. Children who engage in repeated sexualized behaviors with animals or who harm animals, raise concern.

15. *Children sexualize nonsexual things, or interactions with others, or relationships.* For example, the child imagines "she wants to be my girlfriend," or "he is thinking about doing sex" without any observable basis for thinking this. The child sees everyday objects as sexual or sees people as sexual objects.

16. *Sexual behaviors that cause physical or emotional pain or discomfort to self or others.* Children who engage in any behaviors, including sexual behaviors, that induce pain or discomfort to themselves or others, cause concern.

17. *Children who use sex to hurt others.* When sex and pain, sex and disappointment, sex and hurt, sex and jealousy, or sex and other negative emotions and experiences have been paired, the children may use sex as a weapon. Angry sexual

language and gestures as well as sexual touching becomes a way to get back at people. This can be in much the same way as it has been used against them.

18. *When verbal and/or physical expressions of anger precede, follow, or accompany the sexual behavior.* In healthy development, sexual expression and exploration is accompanied by positive emotions. Verbal or physical aggression that accompanies children's sexual behaviors is a learned response to sexuality. In general, children who repeat this behavior have witnessed repeated instances in which verbally and/or physically aggressive behavior has occurred—often in the context of sex. Children may have witnessed their parents or other adults hitting one another when fighting about sexual matters. Some children may have witnessed a parent being sexually misused. Some parents use highly sexual words when verbally assaulting their partners.

Children who have been sexually abused may feel anger and suspicion about all sexual expression. When children associate negative and hostile emotions with sexual behavior, this may be their response to having been coerced, forced, bribed, fooled, manipulated or threatened into sexual contact, or aware of this happening to someone else. When verbal or physical expressions of anger are paired with the child's sexual expression, this is cause for great concern.

When children use bad language it is generally with each other and out of the earshot of adults. If young children are using sexual language in a violent way and directing it at others, this may be cause for concern. (It is important to know the use of sexual or violent language at home.)

19. *Children who use distorted logic to justify their sexual actions. ("She didn't say 'no.' ")* When caught doing something wrong, children often try to make an excuse. When young children make excuses about sexual behaviors that

disregard others' rights and deny any responsibility for their own sexual actions, this raises concern.

20. *When coercion, force, bribery, manipulation, or threats are associated with sexual behaviors.* Healthy sexual exploration may include teasing or daring; unhealthy sexual expression involves the use of emotional or physical force or coercion to engage another child in sexual behavior. Children who engage in coercive sexual behavior may find a child who is emotionally or physically vulnerable to coerce into the sexual behavior. Although infrequent in young children, groups of children may use sex to hurt other children.

Appendix B

How to Use the Behavior Chart

OBJECTIVES

- To assist the children to manage their behavior.
- To provide a tool that will reinforce the behaviors that are important for the children to learn.
- To provide a format for adults to reinforce positive behaviors for the children and highlight negative and disruptive behaviors.

RATIONALE AND PURPOSE

If children with significant behavioral difficulties are going to work together in a group setting, it is generally helpful to have a behavioral system in place prior to the group beginning. When children's behavior becomes the focus of the group's attention, it detracts from the work. Children in therapy for problematic sexual behaviors often have other behaviors that are difficult to manage. Setting up a group structure and a behavioral system provide helpful containment for the children's anxieties.

If a group is to last for many months, it will be useful to start the group with the behavioral program alerting the children to the fact that as they grow more comfortable with the group they will probably no longer need the chart. They will then want to participate and help each other. While they are learning to know each other the chart will be used to help remind them about their behavior.

Frequently, children are not taught to internalize the prohibitions regarding disrupting the group. Their behaviors are always managed via behavioral interventions. When this occurs, the children do not learn to appreciate their own ability to control their behavior and feel proud of their accomplishment. This can be a particular problem in residential treatment where all behaviors are on a contingency management system.

When working with a behavioral system, be careful to be consistent in scoring between the children and across sessions. If you are planning to be more lenient, announce it. Otherwise, determine the criteria for giving and taking away points and stick to it. If the children feel that the criteria are arbitrary, they will feel angry or mistreated. As the children's parents may be inconsistent, the adults must work hard to be very consistent.

USING BEHAVIORAL CHARTS

Materials:

Behavioral charts with different borders

1. A variety of the charts are shown to the children, who each picks one. They can look at the chart to understand how the behavioral system works.

2. There are two different types of categories. Those that add points and those that subtract points. Explain each set of the categories. The first two categories are ones that take away points from the child. A point will be taken away for each occurrence. The first category is very important to the curriculum material. "Space invasion" will be the subject of many of the exercises. Space invasion can be explained as the many ways in which people make others uncomfortable. This can be emotionally, sexually, or physically. The second category "interfering with group work" can be defined in additional ways than those stated on the chart.

The second set of categories adds points to the child's score. The first category is "positive participation." This encourages children to join in the group discussion. It is very important that children participate in the group exercises and discussion, as this will be the way they will learn and the adults will understand the children's thoughts, feelings, and apprehensions. The next category is "active listening." For children who have difficulty speaking in the group but who are clearly listening and attending to the material, this category can net them some points.

Children are encouraged to actively engage in empathic connections with their group members. When they do this, they get points under "Letting someone know you care about their feelings." To encourage the generalization of the material outside the group, children can get points if they use things in the cottage that they learn doing the exercises. When they return to group they can relate incidents in which they showed empathy or incidents in the cottage that relate to the group material. Caregivers may relate incidents in which they have seen children be empathic or use material from group in a helpful way.

3. The points can be an infinite number in all categories except "positive participation" and "active listening."

There are many ways to use the points. It can be agreed that all group members who reach a certain number of points will be able to have a special treat after group. Or that all group members who have a total of a certain number of points will have a special activity at the end of six weeks. There may be a minimum number of points each child has to get in every group in order to have a special treat at the end of the group or the six weeks.

Use the point system to encourage cooperation and learning. If it feels punitive or too restrictive it will not be useful. The point system is a way of reminding the children to focus and of rewarding them for doing it.

4. The points can be given by the adults or by a combination of the adults and the children. In some situations it is helpful for the

children to give themselves the points and then let other members comment on the accuracy of their self-scoring. This encourages the children to pay attention to the other group members' behavior. It can also help children learn how to speak to their fellow group members in a supportive manner. If children do not agree with another child's self appraisal, it can help the children learn to confront the child without hurting the child.

Tendencies by children to want other group members' approval by saying they should have more points than are warranted can be discussed by the adults. If there is any bullying or ganging up on group members through this process, this can be brought to light by the adults. The dynamics of victim and victimizer can arise. Discussing it can be helpful for group learning.

5. As the children coalesce as a group, begin to back the point system down by paying less attention to it.

GROUP CHART

Group Members	Subtract — Space Invasion. (Telling someone how *they* feel. Invading personal space–touching. Making someone uncomfortable by sexual talk or actions.)	Subtract — Interfering with Group Work. (Not staying in your seat, grumpy talk, off topic, distracting.)	Add — Positive Participation in Group.	Add — Active Listening.	Add — Letting Someone Know You Care About His/Her Feelings. (During group.)	Add — Example of How You Used Something You Learned in Group. (Outside of group.)	Total — Total Score
	Infinite	Infinite	Possible=6	Possible=2	Infinite	Infinite	

99

GROUP CHART

Group Members	Subtract	Subtract	Add	Add	Add	Add	Total
	Space Invasion. (Telling someone how *they* feel. Invading personal space—touching. Making someone uncomfortable by sexual talk or actions.)	Interfering with Group Work. (Not staying in your seat, grumpy talk, off topic, distracting.)	Positive Participation in Group.	Active Listening.	Letting Someone Know You Care About His/Her Feelings. (During group.)	Example of How You Used Something You Learned in Group. (Outside of group.)	Total Score
	Infinite	Infinite	Possible=6	Possible=2	Infinite	Infinite	

GROUP CHART — Date _____

Group Members	Subtract Space Invasion. (Telling someone how *they* feel. Invading personal space—touching. Making someone uncomfortable by sexual talk or actions.)	Subtract Interfering with Group Work. (Not staying in your seat, grumpy talk, off topic, distracting.)	Add Positive Participation in Group.	Add Active Listening.	Add Letting Someone Know You Care About His/Her Feelings. (During group.)	Add Example of How You Used Something You Learned in Group. (Outside of group.)	Total Total Score
	Infinite	Infinite	Possible=6	Possible=2	Infinite	Infinite	

101

GROUP CHART

Group Members	Subtract	Subtract	Add	Add	Add	Add	Total
	Space Invasion. (Telling someone how *they* feel. Invading personal space—touching. Making someone uncomfortable by sexual talk or actions.)	Interfering with Group Work. (Not staying in your seat, grumpy talk, off topic, distracting.)	Positive Participation in Group.	Active Listening.	Letting Someone Know You Care About His/Her Feelings. (During group.)	Example of How You Used Something You Learned in Group. (Outside of group.)	Total Score
	Infinite	Infinite	Possible=6	Possible=2	Infinite	Infinite	

GROUP CHART

Group Members	Subtract	Subtract	Add	Add	Add	Add	Total
	Space Invasion. (Telling someone how *they* feel. Invading personal space—touching. Making someone uncomfortable by sexual talk or actions.)	Interfering with Group Work. (Not staying in your seat, grumpy talk, off topic, distracting.)	Positive Participation in Group.	Active Listening.	Letting Someone Know You Care About His/Her Feelings. (During group.)	Example of How You Used Something You Learned in Group. (Outside of group.)	Total Score
	Infinite	Infinite	Possible=6	Possible=2	Infinite	Infinite	

103

Appendix C

Worksheets

WORKSHEET #1

Name:_____ **Date:**_____

Harmful and Hurtful (Attacking)Talk	Saying It Like It Is Without Attacking and Hurting

WORKSHEET #2

Name:_____ **Date:**_____

Harmful and Hurtful (Attacking) Talk	Saying It Like It Is Without Attacking and Hurting	Responding to Harmful and Hurtful Talk

WORKSHEETS #1 and #2 Completed

Name:_____ **Date:**_____

Harmful and Hurtful (Attacking) Talk	Saying It Like It Is Without Attacking and Hurting	Responding to Harmful and Hurtful Talk
"Your breath is kicking like Van Damme."	"Could you please go brush your teeth?"	"Please don't say that to me."
"Oh no, my day is ruined."	"Would you please not yell today."	"Well, you still have a chance to turn it around."
"Why don't you go back where you came from?"	"Why don't you be a little nicer when you come here?"	"This is a nice, beautiful place and I don't want to leave it."
"**Get** in your room **right now**." (YELLING)	"Please go to your room." (not yelling) "Ladies, please go to your room."	"Can you please not yell at me?" "Next time could you please say 'Please go to your room?' "
"Why don't you go home?"	"Please leave me alone."	"I can't go there because I would get hurt there."
"You are the reason I abandoned you."	"I wish I had had enough responsibility and time to take care of you."	"Would you please not tell me all of this is my fault when I'm not responsible for it?"
"I don't care."	"Would you please leave me alone." "I really need some space."	"It seems there is something really bothering you. Can you help me to understand?"
"Leave me alone. Mind your own business."	"I really don't feel like talking now."	"It hurts my feelings when you say that."
"Shut up."	"Please be quiet."	"Please don't talk to me like that."
"Fatso."	"Not to hurt your feelings, but you could lose some weight."	"I know you don't mean to hurt my feelings, but I don't like to talk about how much I weigh. Thank you for your opinion."
"I hate you."	"Sometimes you make me so mad."	"What have I done to make you dislike me?"
"Nobody asked you to get in my conversation."	"Please mind your own business."	"I thought you were talking to me."
"You stink."	"I'm not meaning to be rude, but you smell funny."	"Please don't say my business out loud."

WAYS WE SHOW WE ARE UNCOMFORTABLE

Trying to change the subject.

Looking and feeling nervous.

Blushing.

Leaving the room.

"Uh oh" face.

Scrunching up in a ball.

Becoming very quiet.

Looking around.

Looking down and not speaking.

Rolling eyes.

Staring blankly.

Refusing to answer.

Giggling.

Screaming.

Locking self in closet.

Hiding.

Heart racing, shortness of breath, headache.

Pretending you don't hear.

Playing with your finger, backpack, etc.

Trying to distract the person's attention toward something or somebody else.

Backing away.

WAYS WE SHOW WE ARE UNCOMFORTABLE

WHAT BEHAVIORS ARE SUSPICIOUS?

Someone being really nice–too nice.

Staff going in bedroom with a kid and closing the door.

Being called upstairs by a kid when no one else is up there.

Staff making up excuses to keep a kid alone and separate from other kids.

Someone wants to take you somewhere where no other people are around. "Come in here. I have to talk to you. I have something for you."

Being asked to keep a (bad) secret. If someone would be in trouble if the secret were told, it is a bad secret.

Bribes: Gifts, special favors, special rules from a staff person, or special attention for no good reason.

Threats: "If you don't go AWOL with me, I'll beat you up."

"If you tell, I'll get you at bedtime."

DANGER

"If you don't skip school with me, I'll start a rumor."

"It would be funny if you got jumped after school."

Someone being too silly or goofy, like a drunk person.

Threatening body language.

Invitations such as: "Let's play fight." "Let's play house."

WHAT BEHAVIORS ARE SUSPICIOUS?

QUESTIONS TO ASK MYSELF WHEN I AM UNCOMFORTABLE WITH SOMEONE

Do I trust this person? Do I like this person?

Has this person tricked me before?

Should I go alone with him or her?

Should I answer his or her questions?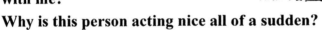

Is this person a friend or faking?

Do I want to play with this person?

Would this person try anything with me?

Why is this person acting nice all of a sudden?

Do I feel comfortable alone with this person?

Is this person acting defensive or getting an attitude?

Is he or she trying to hint about sex?

Do I feel pressured? Do I feel pressured into sex?

Are the questions being asked too personal?

Is the person showing me too much of his or her body?

Am I willing to be sexual just to make a friend?

What do I know about this person that will help me decide if this is all right?

Is the person trying to get me alone? Should I be alone with this person?

Is the person telling me too much personal stuff about himself or herself?

What am I getting into? Is the person mean?

What can I do to make myself feel safer, better, more comfortable, less uneasy?

QUESTIONS TO ASK MYSELF WHEN I AM UNCOMFORTABLE

Index

Page numbers followed by the letter "f" indicate figures.

Abuse
 allegations of, 16-17
 prevention of, 69-82
 protocol for reporting, 1-2
 warnings of, 16-17
Adolescent perpetrators, 70
Adult group members, 7-8
Alertness (exercise), 78-80
Allegations of abuse, 16-17,42
 false, 44
Alternate words for sexual parts,
 65-66
As Boys Grow Up, 19,68
As Girls Grow Up, 19,68
As you grow up (exercise), 68
As You Grow Up, 19,68
Avoiding harmful and hurtful
 communication, 30f,32f

"Bad touch," 36
Behavior chart, 14
 how to use, 95-98
Behavior enforcer, 14
Behavior management, 10
 in group, 13-14
Behavior (suspicious) worksheets,
 110,111
Being alert (exercise), 78-80
Body language, and communication,
 27-28
Body parts, naming (exercise), 64-66

Caregivers, 6
 cottage, 9-10
 immediate, 10
 threatened by curriculum, 12
Characteristics of problematic sexual
 behavior, 86-94
Child group members, 7
Children
 helping other children (exercise), 82
 molesting children, 46,70
 rules to remember, 81
 vulnerable to abuse, 70
Cofacilitators, 8-10
Comforting and soothing
 (communication), 23
Communication. *See also* Harmful
 and hurtful communication
 and body language, 27-28
 examples of, 23-24
 exercises
  a continuum
   of communication I, 22-25
  a continuum
   of communication II, 25-29
  harmful and hurtful
   communications I, 29-31
  harmful and hurtful
   communications II, 31-33
 verbal vs. nonverbal, 3-4
Confusing (communication), 24
Confusing touch, 43
Continuum of communication
 I and II (exercises), 22-29

Cottage caregivers, 6,9-10
Curiosity, sexual, 36
Curriculum
  implementation of, 4-5
  and therapy, 18
  threatening caregiver, 12
  using, 5-6

Differentiating sexual play
    vs. sexual abuse, 51-53

Emotional boundaries, 57
Evaluation, of prevention programs, 1
Examples of communication, 23-24
Examples of threats by
    sex offenders, 77
Exercises
  and abuse prevention
    being alert, 78-80
    children helping other
      children, 82
    figuring out the rules, 80-82
    learning about prevention
      through plays, 71-75
    threats of sex offenders, 75-78
  for communication
    a continuum
      of communication I, 22-25
    a continuum
      of communication II, 25-29
    harmful and hurtful
      communications I, 29-31
    harmful and hurtful
      communications II, 31-33
  for privacy
    personal comfort zones, 58-60
    space invaders, 60-62
  for sexuality
    function of sexual parts, 66-67
    naming body parts, 64-66
    where do I come from?, 67
  for touching
    a continuum of touch I, 39-41

Exercises (*continued*)
    a continuum of touch II, 41-44
    let's talk about touching, 54
    sexual touch, 44-47
Expressing a need
    (communication), 23

False allegations of abuse, 44
Family group session, 17
Feedback, 12
Figuring out the rules
    (exercise), 80-82
Foster home, 2
Function of sexual parts
    (exercise), 66-67

Gathering information, 85-86
Grooming process of sex offenders
    (exercise), 75-78
Group chart (examples of), 99-103
Group home, 2
Group leaders, 8-10
Group meeting
  behavior management in, 13-14
  length of, 12-13
    structuring time, 14-15
  saving information from, 17
Group members, 7-8
Group process, 15
Group size, 13
Group, types of, 17

Harmful and hurtful
    communication, 24
  avoiding, 30f,32f
  I and II (exercises), 29-33
  messages, 29,30f
  responding to, 32,32f
  talk, 31,32f
    worksheets, 105,106,107
Harmful touch, 36,43
Healthy sexual behavior, 85-86
Healthy touch, 36
Helping other children (exercise), 82

Holding hands, 51
Human "private parts," touching, 45

Immediate caregivers, 10
Imparting, personal information, 11
Implementing a curriculum, 4-5
Information gathering process, 85-86
Information from group, saving, 17
Individual group, 17
Intervention issues, 18-19

Knowledge of sex, 63-68

Language usage, 6
Learning about prevention through
    plays (exercise), 71-75
Length, of group meetings, 12-13
Let's talk about touching
    (exercise), 54
Let's Talk About Touching, 20,50
Line staff, 10

Measuring distance, for personal
    privacy, 59-60
Misuse
    allegations of, 16-17
    prevention of, 69-82
Molesting, of children by children, 46
Multifamily group, 17

Naming body parts (exercise), 64-66
Natural sexual behavior, 85-86
Neutral (communication), 24
Neutral touch, 40-41
No communication, 24

Objectives of communication, 21
Ordering further information, 19-20

Out-of-home care
    policies in, 7
    privacy in, 57
    and sex offenders, 76-77
    and touch, 41

Parents, as teachers, 1
People to tell if feeling unsafe, 81
Personal comfort zones
    privacy exercise, 58-60
    realizing that of others, 62
Personal information, imparting, 11
Personal space, 55-62
Physical space requirements, 56-57
Plays, learning prevention through
    (exercise), 71-75
Policies in out-of-home care, 7
Positive touch, 40,41
Post-traumatic stress disorder, 37
Purpose of communication, 21-22
Purpose of touch, 36-38
Prevention programs
    evaluation of, 1
    in school, 1
Prevention of sexual
    misuse/abuse, 17,69-82
Privacy. *See also* Personal space
    exercises
        personal comfort zones, 58-60
        space invaders, 60-62
    in out-of-home care, 57
    and physical boundaries, 56
Private body parts
    alternate words for, 65
    naming, 64-66
    proper names for, 66-67
"Private" signs, 60-61
Problem and solution game cards, 54
Problematic sexual behavior, 86-94
Process, 15
Protocol for reporting abuse, 1-2
PTSD. *See* Post-traumatic stress
    disorder
Purpose, 2-3

Questions to ask when feeling
uncomfortable (worksheets),
78,79,112,113

Rationale for communication, 21-22
Reporting abuse, protocol for, 1-2
Residential Treatment Centers, 2,3,37
"Responding to harmful
and hurtful talk," 32,32f
Reunification services, 17
RTCs. *See* Residential Treatment
Centers
Rules, figuring out, 80-82

Saving information from group
meeting, 17
"Saying it like it is without attacking
and hurting," 32,32f
Scenarios for abuse prevention, 72-75
Self-esteem, 29
Sex offender, 70
grooming of, 75-78
Sexual aspects of a person, 45-46
Sexual behaviors, 85-86
characteristics of problematic,
52-53,86-94
Sexual curiosity, 36
Sexual knowledge, 63-68
Sexual misuse/abuse,
prevention of, 69-82
Sexual parts. *See* Private parts
Sexual play vs. sexual abuse, 49-54
Sexuality and touching, 36,38
children's feelings toward, 86
exercises
a continuum of touch I, 39-41
a continuum of touch II, 41-44
sexual touch, 44-47
Size of group, 13
Space invasion, 55. *See also*
Personal space
exercise, 60-62
Staff members, and touching, 42
Structuring group time, 14-15

Supervision, 11-12
of privacy, 57
Supplementary materials,
ordering, 19-20
Suspicious behaviors
(worksheets), 110-111

Taking care of (communication), 23
Teachers, parents as, 1
Therapy, curriculum, 18
Thoughts with communication, 24-25
Threats of sex offenders
(exercise), 75-78
examples of, 77
Touch, 35-39
exercises
a continuum of touch I, 39-41
a continuum of touch II, 41-44
let's talk about touching, 54
sexual touch, 41-44
holding hands, 51
Types of groups, 17

Uncomfortable
questions to ask when feeling
(worksheets), 78,79,112,113
ways we show we are
(worksheets), 108,109
Using a curriculum, 5-6
Using language, 6

Verbal vs. nonverbal
communication, 3-4
Violating personal space, 61-62
Violent touch, 43
Vulnerable children, 70

Warnings of abuse, 16-17
Ways we show we are uncomfortable
(worksheets), 78,79,108,109
What behaviors are suspicious?, 78,79
Where do I come from? (exercise), 67
Where Do I Come From? (video), 67

Order Your Own Copy of
This Important Book for Your Personal Library!

SEXUAL, PHYSICAL, AND EMOTIONAL ABUSE IN OUT-OF-HOME CARE
Prevention Skills for At-Risk Children

_____ in hardbound at $39.95 (ISBN: 0-7890-0088-1)

_____ in softbound at $17.95 (ISBN: 0-7890-0193-4)

COST OF BOOKS_____

OUTSIDE USA/CANADA/
MEXICO: ADD 20%_____

POSTAGE & HANDLING_____
(US: $3.00 for first book & $1.25
for each additional book)
Outside US: $4.75 for first book
& $1.75 for each additional book)

SUBTOTAL_____

IN CANADA: ADD 7% GST_____

STATE TAX_____
(NY, OH & MN residents, please
add appropriate local sales tax)

FINAL TOTAL_____
(If paying in Canadian funds,
convert using the current
exchange rate. UNESCO
coupons welcome.)

☐ **BILL ME LATER:** ($5 service charge will be added)
(Bill-me option is good on US/Canada/Mexico orders only;
not good to jobbers, wholesalers, or subscription agencies.)

☐ Check here if billing address is different from
shipping address and attach purchase order and
billing address information.

Signature_____

☐ **PAYMENT ENCLOSED: $**_____

☐ **PLEASE CHARGE TO MY CREDIT CARD.**

☐ Visa   ☐ MasterCard   ☐ AmEx   ☐ Discover

Account #_____

Exp. Date_____

Signature_____

Prices in US dollars and subject to change without notice.

NAME_____

INSTITUTION_____

ADDRESS_____

CITY_____

STATE/ZIP_____

COUNTRY_____ COUNTY (NY residents only)_____

TEL_____ FAX_____

E-MAIL_____
May we use your e-mail address for confirmations and other types of information? ☐ Yes   ☐ No

Order From Your Local Bookstore or Directly From
The Haworth Press, Inc.
10 Alice Street, Binghamton, New York 13904-1580 • USA
TELEPHONE: 1-800-HAWORTH (1-800-429-6784) / Outside US/Canada: (607) 722-5857
FAX: 1-800-895-0582 / Outside US/Canada: (607) 772-6362
E-mail: getinfo@haworth.com
PLEASE PHOTOCOPY THIS FORM FOR YOUR PERSONAL USE.

BOF96

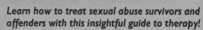